THE SIN OF WIT

THE
SIN
OF
WIT

Jonathan Swift as a Poet

Swift had the sin of wit, no venial crime;
Nay, 'twas affirm'd, he sometimes dealt in rhime;
Humour, and mirth, had place in all he writ:
He reconcil'd divinity and wit.
                    ("The Author upon Himself," 9-12)

Maurice Johnson

GORDIAN PRESS, INC.   1966

Printed in U.S.A. by
EDWARDS BROTHERS, INC.
Ann Arbor, Michigan

ACKNOWLEDGMENTS

My thanks are due to Professor Marjorie Hope Nicolson, Mr. Harold Williams, Professor Herbert Davis, Professor Joseph Wood Krutch, and Mr. Weldon Kees, who took the time to read early drafts of this book in typescript. My chief debt for continued encouragement and advice I owe to Professor James Lowry Clifford of Columbia University. From Professor Lester Middleswarth Beattie, Professor Ricardo Quintana, Professor Gilbert Highet, and Mr. T.S. Eliot, I have received certain materials, information, or suggestions. Nancy Dilworth Johnson and Laurie Johnson have assisted me in various ways. The Pierpont Morgan Library has permitted me to examine manuscripts and letters in Swift's hand. A portion of the Appendix to this book has been published in Modern Language Notes.

Most of the quotations from Swift's poems are based upon texts in the Syracuse University Library: Volumes II (1737), VI (1738), and VIII (1746) of the Works published by George Faulkner in Dublin. For every quotation I have made comparison with the text in Mr. Harold Williams's indispensable annotated edition of the Poems, 1937.

THE SIN OF WIT

JONATHAN SWIFT AS A POET

/

ILLUSTRATIONS

INTRODUCTION

1.

If the reader of poetry is a delicate sounding-board only for parlor sentiment, "beauties," and what he hopes is sublimity, he will feel lamentable rudeness in much of the poetry of Jonathan Swift. Parlor sentiment is turned inside-out or upside-down in Swift's pages, "beauties" prove to be impostors, and sublimity can be a source for mirth. No one disagrees that a very significant type of poetry is breathtaking in loveliness, awakening reverent emotions that soar into the stratosphere. Hardly anyone would disagree either that even in inspired hands this type of poetry often goes wrong: when sublimity turns out to be only dull or full of gas, it is poetry's most obtrusive source of embarrassment. It is, Swift wrote in "An Epistle to a Lady Who Desired the Author to Make Verses on Her, in the Heroick Stile," like a rocket meant to pierce the sky but only bursting into pieces in middle air, falling in a thousand sparkles, and returning dead to earth:

> Thus, shou'd I attempt to climb,
> Treat you in a stile sublime,
> Such a rocket is my Muse;
> Shou'd I lofty numbers chuse,
> E'er I reach'd Parnassus' top
> I shou'd burst, and bursting drop.
> (257-262)

Swift had no mercy for the ambitious scribbler who cried out that he was soaring like a swan while he still fluttered and flopped on the drawingroom carpet:

> And now he spreads his little fans,
> (For all the Muses' geese are swans)
> And borne on Fancy's pinions, thinks,
> He soars sublimest when he sinks . . .
> ("Vanbrug's House," early version, 49-52)

More consistently than his fellow Augustans, the author of *Gulliver's Travels* held the Sublime and Beautiful in doubt and had the audacity to laugh at them when they seemed a fraud. Other members of the Scriblerus Club—dedicated to the ridicule of pedants and correction of false tastes—joined him only occasionally in this crotchety attitude. Gay, for instance, is best known for happy burlesques like *The Beggar's Opera*, but he tried high flights in *Dione* and *The Captives*. Though not quite sure of himself, another Scriblerian, Parnell, wanted to believe with Milton that poetry is a heavenly beneficence: "My God! I think I feel the gift is thine," Parnell wrote hopefully of his own Muse. In "Peri Bathous: or the Art of Sinking in Poetry" Pope formulated rules for Low Verse and ironically told how to mix clouds and billows for a poetic tempest, set fire to a town in rhyme, or put Jupiter "in a ferment." Yet Pope himself attempted some serious flights of imagination. He would not have wished to share Swift's reckless description of his own poetry as

> No thought, no fancy, no *sublime* . . .
> ("To Mr. Delany," 11)

For Thomas Hobbes the sublime consisted of poetical fancy and fury; for Sir William Temple it was that which amazed; and the critic John Dennis, defining it at length at the beginning of the eighteenth century, identified it with "enthusiastick passion." Dennis's enthusiastic passions are six: admiration or wonder, terror, horror, joy, sadness, and desire. He insisted that these emotions are strongest when they rise from enthusiasms predominantly religious.

Now, fanatics, enthusiastic preachers, and excess of religious ecstasy are the subjects of some of Swift's most violent ridicule, especially in *A Tale of a Tub* and *A Discourse Concerning the Mechanical Operation of the Spirit*, when he wickedly describes the preacher's "sublime" snuffling and nose-blowing that pierce the hearts of a simple-minded congregation. Pulpit-enthusiasm for him was merely the art of canting, devoid of wit, humor, or sincerity. Canting seemed to him no more attractive in poetry than in the pulpit.

He scorned poets like Sir Richard Blackmore, who wrote a *Satyr against Wit* and set himself up as a sublime poet, carefully seeking to evoke wonder, terror, joy, and a sense of vastness. Blackmore's poems are heavy-laden with "pure cerulean fields," "waste places," "effulgent emanations," "rolling worlds immense," "heaven's bright towers," and "fierce storms." Despite all his endeavor Blackmore's storms are not very fierce and his towers are not very bright. *The Dunciad* ridicules the braying of this "enthusiast," and in Swift's verses "On Poetry: A Rapsody" poor Blackmore is thrust with a leaden crown into the category of the "low sublime," which is beneath the ridiculous.

At least one of Swift's own poems appears on first examination to suit all the eighteenth-century critical requirements for sublimity of the loftiest kind. Dennis, like Edmund Burke after him, saw terror as a grand emotion and wrote that the greater the terror in a poem, the greater the poem might be. Nothing, he said, neither ruined abbeys nor howling ghosts nor the thought of bodily decay, was so terrible—and sublime—as the idea of an angry God. It is difficult to imagine an angrier God than the Jove of Swift's "Day of Judgement." But Swift deliberately and paradoxically spurns sublimity. By means of a witty stylistic device, in "The Day of Judgement" and other poems, he builds up an effect only to overturn it. He is deliberately anti-"poetic"—opposing insincerity, prettiness, and the false sublime.

2.

Just as sublimity itself in Swift's day had been measured

and weighed and was attempted by recipe, poems were generally written to fit into compartments each unmistakably identified. On each poetic compartment sat a proprietary Muse representing the noble epic, the ode, satire, the elegy, the epistle, the song, pastorals and georgics, imitations and translations, or occasional verse. These genres—and their variations—had forms and patterns based upon respected tradition; there was precedent at hand for almost any poetic expression proper to the Age of Reason. The writer of verses chose the compartment most suited to what he had in mind; and when his verses had been printed, they were read by a public expecting to recognize one of the conventional kinds of poetry. In the early years of the eighteenth century it was even possible to identify the nature of certain poems by their format: broadside elegies and their appended epitaphs were printed in black letter and could not be mistaken, with their mourning margins that showed cross-bones, shrouds, coffins, skeletons, and a "memento mori." The nature of a poem was often explicit in its title: "The Medall: A *Satyre* against Sedition"; "Rural Sports: A *Georgic*, Inscribed to Mr. Pope"; "The Bard: A *Pindaric Ode*"; "*Elegy* Wrote in a Country Church-yard." An eighteenth-century audience, knowing what to look for in verse, required no such explanation as that provided by the publishers of a twentieth-century Baroque Eclogue. "Mr. Auden's latest poem, *The Age of Anxiety*, is an eclogue," the supposedly puzzled reader is informed; "that is to say, it adopts the pastoral convention in which a natural setting is contrasted with an artificial style of diction."

But poets occasionally reminded themselves of the rules. In Restoration days the Earl of Mulgrave's "Essay upon Poetry" had rehearsed the "differing kinds" and "various sorts of verse." Thirty years later there was a similar rehearsal of "all kinds of poetry" in John Gay's "Epistle to Bernard Lintott." Both of them prescribe that the elegy, for instance, must be "of sweet but solemn voice" and must "fill some pages with melodious woe."

Swift, like his fellow-poets, paused to categorize the various sorts of verse. But unlike them he was less concerned with the rules than with the pitfalls of poetry, satirizing contemporary clichés:

> When wretched lovers live on air,
> I beg you'll the *camelion* spare.
>
> . . .
>
> No son of mine shall dare to say,
> *Aurora usher'd in the day....*
>
> . . .
>
> Your tragick heroes shall not rant,
> Nor shepherds use poetick cant....
>
> . . .
>
> If ANNA's happy reign you praise,
> Pray not a word of *halcyon days.*
>
> . . .
>
> When poets soar in youthful strains,
> No *Phaeton* to *hold the reins.*
>   ("Apollo's Edict," 16-17, 20-21,
>   27-28, 44-45, 52-53)

He differed from Mulgrave and Gay by demonstrating the way in which an elegy should *not* be written:

> When *Damon's soul shall take its flight,*
> Tho' poets have the second sight,
> They shall not see a *trail of light:*
> Nor shall the *vapour upwards rise,*
> Nor a *new star* adorn the skies....
>   (33-37)

In the same manner that Swift chaffed what he considered to be the false sublime, he parodied the several fixed kinds of verse fashionable in the eighteenth century. The titles of his poems show that he wrote within the accepted patterns: there are epistles, odes, ballads, elegies, imitations and translations, pastoral dialogues, and occasional verses. But more often than not, the reader soon discovers, it is "A *Satirical* Elegy," "A *Quibbling* Epigram," "A Love Song *in the Modern Taste,*" or "Verses *on I Know Not What.*" His "Famous Prediction of Merlin" is a practical joke that fooled

even Dr. Johnson; and "A Pastoral Dialogue" pitilessly burlesques the elegant diction expected in that kind of poem.

Because burlesque itself was among the "various kinds"
of verse, it too was written according to rules. The reader
of burlesque was almost certain to encounter preposterous
distortions of famous lines of poetry. Swift was outdone only
by Pope in this sort of parody:

> Before their eyes in sudden view appear
> The secrets of the hoary deep....
>> (Milton, *Paradise Lost*, II, 890-891)

> O may she better learn to keep
> Those secrets of the hoary deep!
>> (Swift, "The Lady's Dressing-Room," 97-98)
>>> . . .

> Though deep, yet clear, though gentle, yet not dull ....
>> (Denham, "Cooper's Hill," 191-192)

> Her hands the softest ever felt,
> Tho' cold would burn, tho' dry would melt.
>> (Swift, "Strephon and Chloe," 27-28)
>>> . . .

> 'Tis doubtful which is sea, and which is sky.
>> (Garth, *The Dispensary*, V, 176)

> 'Twas doubtful which was rain, and which was dust.
>> (Swift, "A Description of a City Shower," 26)

3.

Not content with holding the false sublime up to public
ridicule and parodying the several compartments of poetry,
Swift sometimes played frivolous games with the Latinity
that most other poets of his day used solemnly. Toward the
end of his life he liked to address his friends in a kind of
pig-Latin overborne with puns, as in his "Love Song" that
begins "Apud in is almi des ire...." (A puddin' is all my
desire.)

Though he once complained in a letter that "This Virgil
sticks plaguily on my hands," the Latinity in which he was
schooled plagued his verse through "Baucis and Philemon,"

"The Legion Club," and "Verses on the Death of Dr. Swift."
It was not, for instance, the Christian God that he addressed
or referred to in all his poetry, but the Latin Jove (less odd
perhaps than Gerard Manley Hopkins's referring to God as
"Sir"). When he wrote his single poem describing Nature,
it was not in his own language but in the severity of Latin.
His "Carberiae Rupes," 1723, describing the violence of
angry sea and raging wind, has something in common with
Samuel Johnson's calmer Nature poems for which he also
resorted to the cover of Latin, immured against what might
be considered sentimentality.

There is angry indignation like that of Juvenal in "The
Legion Club" and other poems; but Swift's work more often
shares the wit, humor, and felicity of diction to be found in
Horace, from whom some of his most humorous lampoons are
derived. "Had he lived in the same age with Horace," the
Earl of Orrery wrote in his *Remarks upon the Life and Writings of Dr. Jonathan Swift*, "he would have approached nearer
to him, than any other poet." Like Pope and most of his
other contemporaries he appropriated the Odes, Satires, and
Epistles for his own use, paraphrasing and imitating, as some
modern poets have done with the works of Rilke and Baude-
laire.

Schooled like Swift in Latin, attuned to the neo-classical
code, and suspicious of singularity, the eighteenth-century
reader of poetry expected to find reflections of Latinity in a
new miscellany or volume of verses "on Several Occasions."
Swift's imitations of Horace addressed to Harley must have
seemed admirable to such a reader; and even his scatological
"Lady's Dressing-Room" (printed in *The Gentleman's Magazine* opposite a page of statistics on the national debt) must
have seemed properly reminiscent of Juvenal. But the eighteenth-century reader probably saw some rudeness in Swift's
descriptions of Roman goddesses in un-heavenly postures;
his preference for Cloacina over Diana; his rhymes of
"Juno" / "you know," "solum" / "stole 'um," and "Livy" /
"privy"; and his lines "in praes o Molli":

> Mollis abuti,
> Has an acuti.

No lasso finis;
Molli divinis.
Omi de armistres,
Imi na Dis tres;
Cantu disco ver
Meas alo ver.

4.

The Grubstreet hack of William Hogarth's realistic engraving "The Distressed Poet" sits in a miserable garret, his re-
jected manuscript beside him as he desperately writes for
money to pay his landlady and provide food for his family.
This is no more like Swift than are conventional eighteenth-
century engravings that depict poets with garlands at their
feet, Cupids poised above them, and the Muses proffering
wreaths of laurel. Although Swift appears in this Augustan
attitude in the frontispiece to the Dublin edition of his
Poems on Several Occasions, it is hard to believe nowadays
that the engraving was entirely serious in intention, especially since the "Advertisement" to that edition introduces
the poems as consisting "either of humour or satyr, and very
often of both together." More characteristically Swift the
poet would have been shown in the pose that the Earl of
Rochester assumed for his portrait: crowning a long-tailed
monkey with a wreath of bays.

Because Swift was a parodist in verse (as he was in prose),
"serious" poets of the eighteenth century went out of their
way to avoid resembling him. In his essay "Eighteenth-
Century Poetic Diction" Professor Geoffrey Tillotson men-
tions Swift only to say that his insistence upon calling a
spade a spade frightened other neo-classic poets into the
periphrasis of "billowy main," "bleating kind," "scaly
breed," "humble swain," or "enameled plain." Addison
advised in *Spectator* 285 that "a poet should take particular
care to guard himself against idiomatic ways of speaking."
To be idiomatic was exactly what Swift intended in most of
his verses.

Even as a satirist Swift was occasionally an exception in

his age. Professor James Sutherland (*A Preface to Eighteenth Century Poetry*) differentiates Swift from Addison, Steele, Pope, and Fielding, whose satire was intended for readers already convinced of the opinions to be presented. Like Byron and Shaw, of two succeeding centuries, Swift sometimes flew in the face of public opinion. Although he always reminded other writers of their obligations to polite opinion, Swift was, Professor Sutherland concludes, "a law to himself...."

5.

In the science of physics "to sublime" means to pass directly from a solid to an expansive, gaseous state. For poetry to be "sublime" it must have an analogous quality of rising and expanding; and it must to some degree be inflammable. Like his prose, Swift's poetry is solid, concise, intense, and tangible; once touched by the hand, it will almost always change in form, may prove to be a hoax that in turn proves to be deadly serious, or may be ice that scorches; but it remains a solid. This does not, however, mean that it cannot give pleasure; for, being poetry of humor and wit, it both delights and surprises.

CHAPTER ONE

HE SOMETIMES DEALT IN RHIME

1.

PREPARATION FOR POETRY

The seventeenth century was dying when Jonathan Swift was young. Yet he at first identified himself with the dying century, deferentially invoking the metaphysical Muse that had once served Abraham Cowley. In his first published poem, written with Cowley as his model, Swift tenderly addressed a "young and (almost) Virgin-muse," a Muse that toward the middle of the next century, in "Verses on the Death of Dr. Swift," he dismissed as "a jade" worn out through decades of assistance to his wit. When Swift had become an Augustan, he soon found in Cowley a source for parody and irreverent laughter. As neatly as the death of Dryden in 1700 closed the century, Cowley's death in 1667, the same year Swift was born, marked an exchange of the old age for the new.

Throughout his poetic career, at first imitative and then reactionary before it was truly creative, Swift was a self-conscious craftsman. Occasionally he recorded his poetic problems and aspirations, as he did in a long, confessional, discursive letter to his cousin Thomas in May, 1692, in his twenty-fourth year. It is a letter that reveals as much about his early endeavors as do the poems themselves. He has regularly set aside two hours of the morning for writing and revision of his odes, he tells his cousin, and must "alter them a hundred times," although he does not consider himself "a laborious dry writer." In his wish to compose something "easy to be understood" he is self-critical, and he is concerned with the "honesty of poets," believing that the ability to write well necessitates a deserving subject. His ingenuous admission of overfondness for his own lines ("I have a sort of vanity or foiblesse") and his pride in his first published poem reflect a serious effort behind his versifying. And across this letter to his cousin, as well as across the early poems, lie the heavy shadows of Abraham Cowley, "rich Mr. Cowley," the "Pindaric" Cowley he wanted to emulate, and Sir William Temple, whom Swift preferred "to all others at present in England." Not only the idea for the ode to the Athenian Society but even figures of speech in the early poems come in large part from Temple, the founder of the Privy Council and negotiator of the Triple Alliance, who had now retired to his orchards and kept Jonathan Swift as his servant among the pippins, muscadines, apricots, folios, quartos, shell-rock-work, and female relatives at Moor Park. In his *Miscellanea* Temple remarked: "I have had several servants far gone in divinity, others in poetry...."; and when he recommended Swift for employment, he wrote: "I venture to make you the offer of a servant, in case you may have occasion for such a one as this bearer...." The servant—his duties were actually those of a personal secretary—endeavored to please his master and flattered him by repeating his stalest pronouncements and similes.

Cyril Connolly, describing Temple as an old Polonius and the M. de Norpois of his day, attributes his influence on Swift to a kind of auto-suggestion. There was another important influence, however—that of the old Polonius's library, in which Swift read hungrily. In 1697 he kept a list of books he read at Moor Park. Chiefly classical, they included Homer, Virgil, Horace, Lucretius, Petronius, Voiture, Blackmore's *Prince Arthur*, and Hobbes's translation of Thucydides. In 1697, too, he wrote most of those remarkable fables called

A Tale of a Tub and *The Battle of the Books*, in which every page, through allusion, parody, or imitation, reflects hours spent in the library. Among the Ancients and Moderns he ranged against each other in the famous "battle" were Aesop, Homer, Virgil, Aristotle, and Pindar; Cowley, Davenant, Denham, Wesley, Blackmore, and Dryden (with a helmet "nine times too large for the head"). Missing from these lists is the name of one writer significant in the study of Swift's poetry. In these early years, when he was receiving his M.A. from Oxford, being ordained a priest, returning intermittently to Moor Park, and trying to find his place in the world, he may already have known the poetry of Samuel Butler. It is the poetry most like his own of later years. And he is supposed to have been able, as an old Dean, to recite all of Butler's *Hudibras*. There is no record of his ability to do this with the work of any other poet, ancient or modern.

The "Ode to the Athenian Society," as Swift wrote in the letter to his cousin, was "rough drawn in a week, and finished in two days after." It was addressed to the anonymous writers for the *Athenian Gazette*, a weekly periodical that professed to answer all queries submitted to it. With a prefatory letter, in which Swift hinted at encouragement from Temple, unnamed, the poem was published in a supplement to the fifth volume of the *Gazette* early in 1692. It was Swift's first appearance in print, and probably his least attractive effort. "The Ramble," mentioned in the letter to his cousin, has been lost, along with another piece called "The Poet"; and although two versions of an ode to King William have been attributed to Swift, there is no absolute proof of his authorship. The early poems that can definitely be established, then, are the "Ode to the Athenian Society," the "Ode to Sir William Temple," the "Ode to Dr. William Sancroft," "To Mr. Congreve," and "Occasioned by Sir W(illiam) T(emple)'s Late Illness and Recovery." Of these only the three entitled "Ode" are in the rhetorical, irregular "Pindaric" form borrowed from Cowley. Heroic couplets are used for the poem to Congreve and that purporting to celebrate Temple's recovery from illness. Only the ode in the *Athenian Gazette* was published in Swift's lifetime.

Without much coherence the "Ode to the Athenian Society"
rants about Swift's own poetic Muse, modern pedantry, and
the world's natural decay, which will bring disintegration of
even the brilliant Athenian Society. These "exalted men,/
Who have well studied in the world's disease" will be succeeded by "Gothic swarms" from "Ignorance's universal
North," a "Careless and ignorant posterity..." Imagery in
the poem is that of inevitable wasting away: with every pass-
ing age Philosophy is less certain; Learning and Wit are
fleeting and vain; winter sun is followed by "the long and
gloomy night"; and every noble work is doomed to "fall at
last to interest, folly, and abuse." This is an understandable
point of view for Sir William Temple, whose Privy Council
had failed, whose Triple Alliance had disintegrated, whose
only son had committed suicide, and who now consoled himself by fighting decay in his orchards. There is Temple's
voice more surely than his servant Swift's in the delineation
of inevitable darkness and disaster.

Again, in the "Ode to the Honourable Sir William Temple,"
it is less the voice of young Swift than of the old ambassador
that reminiscently exclaims:

> Great God! (said I) what have I seen!
> On what poor engines move
> The thoughts of monarchs, and designs of states...
> (103-105)

Dedicated to the "pleasures of retreat," well-groomed plum
trees, woods, vales, and peace, this ode is an oddly arranged
bouquet of blandishments for the Great Man who had retired
from the ugly scrabble of politics to cultivate his prose-style
in leisurely essays "Upon the Gardens of Epicurus" and
"Of Health and Long Life." It is a versification of Temple's
own reasons for abandoning public office, telling how he
wished to secure for himself the peace he had tried to give
his country. Nine lines from the poem have modern interest,
because out of all Swift's early poems they seemed to W.B.
Yeats a marked exception. In conversation concerning Swift,

Yeats called the attention of Harold Williams to the following passage:

> But what does our proud ign'rance Learning call,
>   We odly Plato's paradox make good,
> Our knowledge is but mere remembrance all,
>   Remembrance is our treasure and our food;
> Nature's fair table-book our tender souls
> We scrawl all o'er with old and empty rules,
>   Stale memorandums of the schools;
> For Learning's mighty treasures look
>   In that deep grave a book...
>
>   (28-36)

Temple in retirement, looking back on his years of activity, might himself have written that "knowledge is but mere remembrance all."

Throughout the twelve stanzas of the third "Pindaric," the uncompleted "Ode to Dr. William Sancroft, Late Archbishop of Canterbury," there is a well-defined set of images. Sun is contrasted with cloud, light with darkness, and dazzle with blindness. In the "dusky shade" of this world there is no "brighter pattern" of Truth than Dr. Sancroft (whom Dryden in *Absalom and Achitophel* had called "Zadock the priest"). He is like an unseen star shedding "his sacred influence here." In Swift's eleventh stanza the sun-and-light imagery becomes a blaze: Sancroft's "lustre" shows "glimm'rings of the prelate glorify'd." He is compared to the evening sun "behind a golden cloud" that leaves a "daz'ling glory": "No deflower'd eye can face the naked light..." This imagery, too, as in the "Ode to the Athenian Society," seems borrowed, belonging here more to Milton and Cowley than to Swift. Though obviously imitative, the poem seems more accomplished than Thomas Flatman's "Pindaric" ode also addressed to Dr. Sancroft. It is, as a matter of fact, no clumsier than most of the odes of Cowley, Flatman, Congreve, Addison, and Pope. Dryden's are the only real exception. T.S. Eliot has remarked that, although the Pindaric ode cannot be proved absolutely impossible in English, it has almost always turned out dismal. For Swift to begin his career with an unwieldy vehicle, first trying his skill in a doomed medium, was as hopeless as the project Lemuel Gulliver observed in the Academy in Lagado, for extracting sunbeams out of cucumbers.

Later, in "Directions for a Birth-day Song" and "On Poetry: A Rapsody" he maliciously described the antics a poet must perform to secure patronage, preferment, a laureateship, or a guinea in the hand. Like other odes of his time Swift's were probably intended as a means to an end, political when they flattered the King or Sir William Temple, religious when they praised Dr. Sancroft. Simultaneously with his dropping of the "Pindaric" form, he fixed upon a new goal, neither the court nor the church, but the World of Wits. His younger schoolfellow, William Congreve, was already, ahead of him, a member of that world, and Swift evidently hoped now to join him. "To Mr. Congreve," written in November, 1693, could serve as his means of entrance: its couplets would be printed with Congreve's second comedy, *The Double-Dealer*, and would introduce Swift's name to fashionable society and Grubstreet alike. But the rhymed epistle prefixed to the first edition of that play in 1694 was not Swift's. It was, instead, John Dryden's expert, gracious acknowledgement of Congreve's genius—the old dean-of-the-poets' welcome to a young rival: "To My Dear Friend Mr. Congreve, on His Comedy, Call'd, The Double-Dealer." Before the time came for his epistle to be printed, Swift himself had commanded the world of the Wits and had been dead for over fifty years. Even then nobody had much good to say for it. Only one of its couplets, Juvenalian and anticipatory with its "hate," "sin," "folly," and "lash" that reappear in later poems, seemed worthy of the terrible Dean:

> My hate, whose lash just heaven has long decreed
> Shall on a day make sin and folly bleed . . .
>
> (133-134)

Nowadays, however, "To Mr. Congreve" is properly regarded as Swift's first step toward mature, characteristic accomplishment in either poetry or prose, and thus occupies an important place in the chronology of his works. With a description of a contemptible little fop, who has returned from

London as a "finish'd spark" and self-designated judge of
taste, the poem whips out at the whole tribe of town critics.
Most of the themes important in *A Tale of a Tub*, *Gulliver's
Travels*, and the later poems appear here, only half realized
but already effective. Émile Pons in his exhaustive *Jeunesse
de Swift*, which long ago should have been published in
translation, has noted some of these themes: the same hate
for pedantry and rules that flashes through *A Tale of a Tub*;
the Yahoo-imagery of "odious smell"; the same true satirical
manner of poems like the "Epistle to a Lady" and "On
Poetry: A Rapsody"; and, most significant to Dr. Pons, a
Swiftian mythology, "le mythe animal" of the Houyhnhnms
and "The Beasts Confession." All these themes appear in
a passage printed in Geoffrey Grigson's interesting anthology
Before the Romantics. Under the title of "The Animal Critics"
this excerpt from the poem "To Mr. Congreve" seems dis-
tinctly better, as a sustained creative effort, than the particular verses by Dryden, Defoe, Tom Brown, and Elizabeth
Rowe, among which it stands:

> What northern hive pour'd out these foes to wit?
> Whence came these Goths to overrun the pit?
> How would you blush the shameful birth to hear
> Of those you so ignobly stoop to fear;
> For, ill to them, long have I travell'd since
> Round all the circles of impertinence,
> Search'd in the nest where every worm did lie
> Before it grew a city butterfly;
> I'm sure I found them other kind of things
> Than those with backs of silk and golden wings;
> A search, no doubt, as curious and as wise
> As virtuosoes' in dissecting flies;
> For, could you think? the fiercest foes you dread,
> And court in prologues, all are country-bred;
> Bred in my scene, and for the poet's sins
> Adjourn'd from tops and grammar to the inns;
> Those beds of dung, where schoolboys sprout up beaus
> Far sooner than the nobler mushroom grows:
> These are the lords of the poetic schools,
> Who preach the saucy pedantry of rules;

Those pow'rs the criticks, who may boast the odds
O'er Nile, with all its wilderness of gods;
Nor could the nations kneel to viler shapes,
Which worship'd cats, and sacrific'd to apes;
And can you think the wise forbear to laugh
At the warm zeal that breeds this golden calf?

(83-108)

Here, to defend wit against its enemy the Critic, Swift compares him to a worm, a cat, an ape, and a golden calf; even
a squatting mushroom has more nobility than he. The corus-
cating city butterfly is reminded that he has only recently
left the barnyard, a scene from which Swift often drew satirical imagery. The beaux who sprout from "beds of dung" are
like the "gaudy" female "tulips rais'd from dung" in the
famous "Lady's Dressing-Room," four decades later: of all
Swift's images and symbols—wind, clothing, the barnyard,
dressing-rooms, and beasts, for instance—those pertaining
to excrement are his most constant. Here too, in this early
poem, are a swipe at "pedantry of rules," as in the "Di-
gression" to *A Tale of a Tub*, and a side-blow at virtuosos,
as in the Laputan parodies of the Royal Society. Not all this
passage from "To Mr. Congreve" is forward-looking, however.
The Goths pouring from a "northern hive" are the same
"Gothic swarms" that came out of "Ignorance's universal
North" in the "Ode to the Athenian Society." They are very
likely the same "Gothic swarms" with their "shades of ignorance" that Sir William Temple described in his essay
"Of Poetry."

When Swift reread the lines of his verses "To Mr. Congreve," he may have imagined himself equal to Cowley
("when I write what pleases me I am Cowley to myself," he
had confessed to his cousin); or he may have been discouraged. For in December, 1693, in verses "Occasioned by
Sir W(illiam) T(emple)'s Late Illness and Recovery," he dismissed his Muse. Suddenly desperate and disgusted, he vowed
never to woo the tyrant Muse again:

Malignant goddess! bane to my repose,
Thou universal cause of all my woes . . .

Madness like this no fancy ever seiz'd,
Still to be cheated, never to be pleas'd;
Since one false beam of joy in sickly minds
Is all the poor content delusion finds.——
There thy enchantment broke, and from this hour
I here renounce thy visionary pow'r;
And since thy essence on my breath depends,
Thus with a puff the whole delusion ends.

(81-82, 147-154)

Trying to make a career of poetry, Swift had needed a firmer guide than his own admiration for lumpish odes or his wish to please his aphoristic old employer, Sir William Temple. The criticism that finally came was not a guiding hand but a hard push off a cliff, in Dryden's judgment that he would never be a poet. After the renunciation of his Muse, more than five years passed before he wrote any poetry that he preserved. And then it was the antithesis of the "Pindaric": it took the form of a jingling lampoon in "The Problem," or it was the pleasant doggerel of "Mrs. Harris's Petition," or it was a ballad to the tune of "Cutpurse." There were even *vers de société* in "Apollo Outwitted," addressed to Mrs. Finch, who became the Countess of Winchilsea, and in the lines "To Mrs. Biddy Floyd." There were rhymed jokes like "An Elegy on Mr. Partrige" and "A Famous Prediction of Merlin, the British Wizard; Written above a Thousand Years Ago, and Relating to this Present Year."

All this is casual, sometimes careless, occasional verse that is obviously not intended to have a place in a career dedicated to poetry. That career seems to have been abandoned. But in "Baucis and Philemon" and "A Description of the Morning," both published in 1709, there is the professional poet's sureness of touch. In both these poems there is the pattern and type of wit that Swift perfected and that hardly anyone has had the wit to imitate. Because it is half reactionary and half creative, written with wit that has not quite found itself, "A Description of the Morning" is a useful poem for examination. It represents a transitional phase in Swift's writing of poetry.

2.

"A DESCRIPTION OF THE MORNING"

"A Description of the Morning" has usually been considered of more interest biographically than as a metrical accomplishment. It was first published in Swift's forty-first year, while he was in London on church business as a representative of the Irish clergy. His *Tale of a Tub* and *Battle of the Books* had been published anonymously five years before, and seventeen years were to pass before the publication of *Gulliver's Travels*. In 1709, at the time of "A Description of the Morning," Swift was entering a period of fame and excitement. Now he was perhaps best known as the perpetrator, in his "Bickerstaff" papers, of the most convulsing practical joke of the decade; and within a year and a half he was to be transformed forever from a rhyme-making priest into the king of the Wits. Temporarily, too, he was to be a powerful figure in English politics. In 1709 he wrote a gossipy account of his London literary and political activities in a letter to Col. Robert Hunter, a prisoner in France. It is a letter familiarly concerned with Grubstreet, St. James's Coffeehouse, and the vogue of operas. It wishes ill luck for the Duke of Marlborough, refers to Whigs, Tories, and friends in the Ministry, and speaks of literary men like "Namby-Pamby" Philips, Steele, and Addison ("I am now with Mr. Addison, with whom I have fifty times drunk your health since you left us"). Swift was near the center of things.

In 1709 Queen Anne was in the seventh year of her reign, Samuel Johnson was born, Henry Fielding was two years old, young Pope was writing his "Essay on Criticism," and Steele, taking suggestions from Swift, founded the *Tatler*. It was, indeed, in the ninth issue of the *Tatler*, for April 30, that "A Description of the Morning" first appeared, with an introduction by "Isaac Bickerstaff." The poet, this introduction says, "described things exactly as they happen: he never forms fields, or nymphs, or groves, where they are not; but makes the incidents just as they really appear. For an example of it; I stole out of his manuscript the following lines: they are a description of the morning, but of the morning in town; nay, of the morning at this end of town, where my kinsman at present lodges." This could serve as an introduction to all the rest of Swift's poetry to come; his attempt to combine sense with wit left little place for the stage-scenery of "fields, or nymphs, or groves."

At first glance, Swift seems to have provided no more than a fairly interesting, particularized eighteenth-century scene in his "Description of the Morning." Unlike the verses on his death and the verses to Stella it is not self-consciously personal; unlike his "Legion Club" and "Lady's Dressing-Room" it does not make the reader's hair stand on end. It is a realistic set-piece. It might conceivably have been the text for Hogarth's "Morning," which shows the Begging Crone, the Loose Girl, the Persistent Rake, the Shivering Page, and the Old Maid against a background of snowy pavement, dark buildings, and darker morning sky. Hogarth drew these type-figures and symbols in a style that is witty, ironic, conversational, and full of surprising contrasts; so that no matter how didactic his purpose or how dreadful or commonplace his details, the picture affords pleasure to the eye. Swift's style in his poetry is a counterpart to this: his type-pictures and symbols are often conventional, ready-made ones wittily placed in a new relationship or unexpectedly altered. In "A Description of the Morning," although the subject itself is ready-made, the general texture of the poem, in contrast, is unconventional and anti-"sublime."

As in Hogarth's chilly morning scene, Swift's picture is that of stairways, gateways, and the street, where a few hackney-coaches show that another workday is at hand. Despite the title of the poem, there is no description of Nature. The maid, the apprentice, and the schoolboy dominate the scene, with the mop, old broom, and satchel of books that serve as symbols for their place in life. The people in the poem do not look forward to a day that promises satisfaction or romance: morning means only the end of the night's pleasures if there were any, the return to menial tasks, the resuming of responsibilities and involvements, and for some the jail, or—for the schoolboy just as confining—the classroom.

The Slipshod 'Prentice, the Small-Coal Man, the Dun-Bearers, Brick-Dust Moll, and the Watchful Bailiffs of the poem are un-"poetic" symbols standing for all the workaday creatures who appear with every dawn. They represent a disenchanted idea of Morning—*the* morning, as the title states. Because it is not merely *a* morning that Swift describes, the poem becomes a statement of a point of view, a way of looking at life, and an attitude: as he does elsewhere more violently, he says here that life is an experience more likely to be routine and stupid than a romantic picnicking. And he expresses this attitude, paradoxically, by means of wit that implies an enjoyment of life.

The true wit of such a poem as "A Description of the Morning" issues from its surprising distortion of familiar poetic form and language. Here Swift mocks the elaborate descriptions of time-points (dawn, midnight, etc.) which appear in Greek, Roman and modern classicizing poetry: the cliché "Now Aurora had left the bed of Tithonus" becomes "Now Betty from her master's bed had flown" in Swift's parody. Parody of "poetic" diction grins out from almost every line of Swift's poems like "A Description of the Morning." That particular piece leaves a commonplace impression—on first reading—largely because it has the appearance of a hundred other eighteenth-century verses which go something like this: "Milady twirls her fan with dext'rous airs,/ Prepar'd to make her entry down the stairs. . ." or "The parson now his flock returning sees. . ." Swift's poem does not sound quite like that: he has made witty substitutions in the old familiar phrases and laughs at other poetry while he is writing a poem of his own. The reader sees upon examination that "milady" has been metamorphosed into a scrub-girl, the "fan" is a mop, and the "parson" has become a jailer waiting for his wards:

> Now Moll had whirl'd her mop with dext'rous airs,
> Prepar'd to scrub the entry and the stairs.
> . . .
> The turn-key now his flock returning sees,
> Duly let out a-nights to steal for fees.
>   (7-8, 15-16)

A Description of the Morning

Now hardly here and there a hackney-coach
Appearing show'd the ruddy morn's approach:
Now Betty from her master's bed had flown,
And softly stole to discompose her own.
The slip-shod 'prentice from his master's door
Had par'd the dirt and sprinkled round the floor.
Now Moll had whirl'd her mop with dext'rous airs,
Prepar'd to scrub the entry and the stairs.
The youth with broomy stumps began to trace
The kennel-edge where wheels had worn the place.
The small-coal man was heard with cadence deep;
Till drown'd in shriller notes of chimney-sweep.
Duns at his lordship's gate began to meet;
And brick-dust Moll had scream'd thro' half a street.
The turn-key now his flock returning sees,
Duly let out a-nights to steal for fees.
The watchful bailiffs take their silent stands;
And school-boys lag with satchels in their hands.

Characteristic though most of the poem is, it very likely
reflects the hand of Addison alongside Swift's. Addison wrote
of Swift as "the greatest genius of his age," but took it for
granted that he should criticize, refine, or perhaps even re-
write his friend's metrical compositions. His changes for
"Baucis and Philemon" were numerous and always directed
toward correctness and propriety. It is possible that the heroic
couplets in "A Description of the Morning" were the suggestion of Addison; and it is interesting to consider whether the
poem might not have been racier and stronger if written in the
four-stress poetical line Swift had already taken for his own
use. But as in "A Description of a City Shower," "The Author
upon Himself," and two or three of the adaptations from
Horace, Swift's heroic couplets here are no Iron Maiden in
which the poem is clamped. There are everywhere adjust-
ments, loosenings, and pressures to make the meter fit the
mood.

The first two lines of "A Description of the Morning" set

the basic metrical pattern of iambic pentameter and closed
couplets. In the third line, however, there is no strong accent
on the word "from," where it would naturally fall, and the
line moves more rapidly to suggest the haste of Mrs. Betty.
In the thirteenth and sixteenth lines there are departures from
the metrical norm of the poem in "Duns" and "Duly": instead
of the regular iambic opening, the accent falls on the first
syllable in these lines. Throughout the poem there is a marked
secondary accent in the unusual number of compound words—
in "small-coal," "brick-dust," "turn-key," and "school-
boys" especially. Half the lines in the poem deviate from the
basic metrical pattern.

In the line "Now MOLL had whirl'd her MOP with dext'rous
airs," there is conscious manipulation of sound. There is not
only alliteration in "Moll" and "mop," but there is assonance
of the accompanying vowel, so that the interplay of these
similar-sounding words gives an effect of action to the word
"whirl'd" that is between them. Though the poem is rich with
alliteration, it is not always seriously employed. The ugly,
asthmatic first line is surely intended to give the clue to the
parody to follow:

Now HARDly HERE and there a HACKney-coach . . .

Beyond those that have been noted, there are other effects of
sound that were very likely conscious ones, such as the
repetition in "TURN-key" and "reTURNing" in the fifteenth
line, or the more subtle, less certain echo in "ApPEARing,"
"Had PAR'D," and "PrePAR'D" in lines two, six, and eight.

The line "And school-boys lag with satchels in their
hands," with which "A Description of the Morning" concludes, is admirable for its easy, unobtrusive handling of
meter and sound-combinations. After the descriptions of pre-
dawn and early-morning activities in the poem, the appearance
of the schoolboys marks a kind of finality: daytime has now
arrived. The line moves slowly, with triple-stress on "school-
boys lag" and repetition of a in "And," "lAg," "sAtchels,"
and "hAnds." It is a line perennial in poetry. In "The Morning Quatrains" Charles Cotton had preceded Swift with "The
slick-fac'd school-boy satchel takes,/ And with slow pace

small riddance makes" (65-66). Robert Blair followed with a
less memorable version: "The school-boy, with his satchel
in his hand" ("The Grave," 58). Horace had written it as
"*Laevo suspensi loculos tabulamque lacerto*" (S.1.6.74).
It is best known in the blank verse of Shakespeare's *As You
Like It*, where Jaques makes it "And then the whining school-
boy, with his satchel" (II,vii,145).

Thus, in "A Description of the Morning" the final line
comes out of poetic tradition. It seems admirable and memorable in a way not characteristic of the rest of the poem or of
Swift's poetry in general. Here he has suddenly abandoned his
theme of parody—or at least he has not heightened it as a
final line requires. In other poems, including some of his
most accomplished ones, it is the final line, rushing the reader back to earth with a somersault, that brings the whole effect
of parody and wit. In this poem, written with Addison at hand,
Swift breaks almost entirely, but not quite, from the tradition
he had tried to follow in his "Pindaric" odes. He had already
written his wonderful burlesque of Ovid; but even "Baucis
and Philemon" lacks the audacity of "The Place of the
Damn'd," "The Day of Judgement," "The Legion Club,"
and "Verses on the Death of Dr. Swift."

"A Description of the Morning" is in itself a good poem
that does not wither under close scrutiny. It is, moreover, the
best example of Swift's poetry in an important state of trans-
formation. It already shows the mark of the sin of wit.

3.

"ON POETRY: A RAPSODY"

Written almost a quarter of a century later than the "Morning," "On Poetry: A Rapsody" is representative of Swift's
most mature and sustained satire. It is one of his chief claims
to the title of poet, and is a good introduction to the prosody,
diction, and imagery of his most highly accomplished verse.
To Goldsmith, in *The Beauties of English Poesy*, it seems
"one of the best versified poems in our language, and the
most masterly production of its author." It is Swift's own
Art of Poetry, "Essay on Criticism," and *Dunciad* combined.

Craik says in his *Life of Swift* that "Pope's highest efforts seem weak and almost tame" when compared with "On Poetry: A Rapsody," which "stands side by side with Pope's *Epistle to Augustus*, and transcends the latter in its force of sweeping sarcasm." Swift's satire was so powerful, and his political allusions were so vexing in high places, that after the poem was published, at the end of 1733, his London publisher and the unfortunate Mrs. Barber, who had brought the poem from Dublin, were both imprisoned for a year. Walpole, who had been satirized in a passage beginning "Now sing the Minister of State," issued a warrant for arrest of the author; but when he was told that an army of ten thousand men would be required to lay hands on the Dean in Dublin, he withdrew the order. The poem was considered subversive and dangerous to the welfare of the state. Its title, ironically subheaded "A *Rapsody*," is obviously intended to vex and mock.

There are three main divisions in the poem. First, there is Swift's cynical advice to would-be poets (1-232); next, literary critics and all the inhabitants of Grubstreet ("jobbers in the poet's art") receive a trouncing (233-404); and finally there is the ironical praise, sneering at Monarch and Minister of State, that annoyed Walpole (405-494). In general the lines are remarkably clear and brisk-moving. They do not, like some of the lines of *The Dunciad*, cause the reader to nod, stretch, yawn, and doze along with Pope's heroes; nor do they require an encyclopedic gloss like that appended to the longer poem. Writing to Pope about *The Dunciad*, Swift had remarked: "How it passes in Dublin, I know not yet, but I am sure it will be a great disadvantage to the poem, that the persons and facts will not be understood till an explanation comes out, and a very full one." Now, working with material similar to Pope's, he was allusive but almost never obscure.

Posing as "an old experienc'd sinner" instructing a laureate-in-the-making, Swift is mild and playful at first. He presents a formula for composition of dull poetry:

> Blot out, correct, insert, refine,
> Enlarge, diminish, interline;
> Be mindful, when invention fails,
> To scratch your head, and bite your nails.

> Your poem finish'd, next your care
> Is needful, to transcribe it fair.
> In modern wit all printed trash, is
> Set off with num'rous breaks——and dashes——
>
> To statesmen wou'd you give a wipe,
> You print it in *Italick Type.*
> When letters are in vulgar shapes,
> 'Tis ten to one the wit escapes:
> But when in CAPITALS exprest,
> The dullest reader smoaks a jest:
> Or else perhaps he may invent
> A better than the poet meant,
> As learned commentators view
> In Homer more than Homer knew.
>   (87-104)

Swift assures his "young beginner" that this first attempt
at poetry will be abused by all the critics. He can, however,
line a trunk with his poem and try again a second time and a
third:

> But first with care employ your thoughts,
> Where criticks mark'd your former faults:
> The trivial turns, the borrow'd wit,
> The similes that nothing fit;
> The cant which ev'ry fool repeats,
> Town-jests, and coffee-house conceits;
> Descriptions tedious, flat and dry,
> And introduc'd the Lord knows why...
> Or oft when epithets you link,
> In gaping lines to fill a chink;
> Like stepping stones to save a stride,
> In streets where kennels are too wide:
> Or like a heel-piece to support
> A cripple with one foot too short:
> Or like a bridge that joins a marish
> To moorlands of a diff'rent parish.
> So have I seen ill-coupled hounds,
> Drag diff'rent ways in miry grounds.
> So geographers in Afric-maps

> With savage-pictures fill their gaps;
> And o'er unhabitable downs
> Place elephants for want of towns.
>   (149-156, 167-180)

Swift is almost at his best in this parody of poetic epithets, where his congregation of ineptitudes—stepping-stones, a cripple's heel-piece, a bridge, hounds, and elephants on a map—have the sound of many a poet's serious and sad attempt at brilliant figures of speech. Though he remains always level-voiced, like the disillusioned "old experienc'd sinner" he professes to be, his irony becomes sharp and his wit becomes merciless as the poem continues. It is exactly because the tone is so constantly level and chilly that "On Poetry: A Rapsody" seemed unbearably insulting to Walpole and the others it named.

The second division of the "Rapsody" is, like *The Dunciad*, a personal attack upon certain poets and critics. Both Pope and Swift assumed a kind of critical infallibility, at the same time scorning such an assumption in other writers. Moreover, they both felt contempt for all "jobbers in the poet's art" who depended upon publication for their bread and butter. In Swift this contempt was unreasonable; but in Pope it was indefensible, because his livelihood, like that of the "jobbers," in part depended upon successful publication.

Advising his "young beginner" of the tricks of the critic's trade, Swift makes side-remarks about Rymer, Dennis, Dryden, Cibber, Flecknoe, Howard, Blackmore, Grimston, Welsted, Concannen and Smythe. These are, for the most part, names with which Pope had played. Indeed, in this section of Swift's poem there is the footnote: "*Vide* The Treatise on the Profound, and Mr. Pope's *Dunciad.*" But Swift is not imitative here. Whereas *The Dunciad* is a memorial to dullness, ignorance, and universal darkness, "On Poetry: A Rapsody" is witty and bright. It is distinguished by clever, easy generalizations of a kind that cannot be found in *The Dunciad:*

> Hobbes clearly proves that ev'ry creature
> Lives in a state of war by nature.
> The greater for the smaller watch,

But meddle seldom with their match.
A whale of moderate size will draw
A shole of herrings down his maw.
A fox with geese his belly crams;
A wolf destroys a thousand lambs.
But search among the rhiming race,
The brave are worried by the base.
If, on Parnassus' top you sit,
You rarely bite, are always bit:
Each poet of inferior size
On you shall rail and criticize;
And strive to tear you limb from limb,
While others do as much for him.

(319-334)

This passage has the same joining of felicity and cynicism to be found in the maxims of La Rochefoucauld. In "Verses upon the Death of Dr. Swift" the text is taken from La Rochefoucauld himself. Here it is Hobbes whose philosophy is adapted to a brilliant description of the biting that is habitual among "the rhiming race." There is simple effectiveness in the consistent figure of speech that contrasts the poet with the whale, herrings, fox, and wolf; it was just such a figure of speech that Swift had recommended by implication in his parody of jumbled epithets, earlier in the poem. If the sixteen lines of this passage seem too simple and easy to be great poetry, it must be remembered that the appearance of easiness had been cultivated and perfected for over a quarter of a century. In Swift's early odes there were the complications, obscurities, and flights that are absent here; but there was pretty certainly no great poetry in the early odes.

The best-known lines from the poem, and perhaps the only lines by Swift that have become common property in recitation books and collections of old saws, are those that describe the hierarchies of small critics. They are lines so familiar that they are usually disassociated from Swift's name. Miss Marjorie Nicolson suggests that they are borrowed from the microscopical literature of the period, in which fleas and lice were fashionable subjects for poetry:

> The vermin only teaze and pinch
> Their foes superior by an inch.
> So, nat'ralists observe, a flea
> Hath smaller fleas that on him prey,
> And these have smaller yet to bite 'em,
> And so proceed *ad infinitum:*
> Thus ev'ry poet in his kind,
> Is bit by him that comes behind...
>   (335-342)

In its final division "On Poetry: A Rapsody" turns to pure burlesque. Swift had called court-poetry a prostitution of the Muse's name and had censured the laureate Cibber for his "annual birth-day strains." Now he produces two court-poems of his own, of a kind bold enough to warrant his arrest. For thirty lines he describes the royal family in language that is full of irony. To Professor Quintana this passage seems as intense as anything in Byron's *Vision of Judgment.* It makes George II "the conqu'ring hero" and his royal consort the "perfect goddess born and bred." Adulatory phrases expected of a lackey laureate become simpering and ridiculous in Swift's parody:

> The remnant of the royal blood,
> Comes pouring on me like a flood.
> Bright goddesses, in number five;
> Duke William, sweetest prince alive.
>   (437-440)

In twenty-four succeeding lines Sir Robert Walpole is extravagantly praised for the virtues he had never had:

> In all affairs thou sole director,
> Of wit and learning chief protector;
> Tho' small the time thou hast to spare,
> The Church is thy peculiar care.
>   (449-452)

Remarkably sustained through hundreds of lines, the poem terminates humorously in a cluster of dashes, italics, asterisks, and Latin footnotes.

4.

CRAFTSMANSHIP IN THE POEMS

Through the irony, parody, and satire of his "Rapsody" and similar works, Swift stated his poetic credo. He thought he was a judge of good poetry: proof of that lies in his contemptuous and critical parodies of poetry he knew was bad. But he was not always contemptuous. He took the time to write letters of advice to would-be poets he had never seen, and he read through his friends' verses, meticulously noting down their slips and stumblings. When, for example, he was an old man and Pope a poet of reputation, he wrote in detail to point out, after expressing general admiration, the weaknesses in Pope's epitaph on Gay: "The beginning of the last line, 'striking their aching bosoms.' Those two participles come so near, and sounding so like, I could wish them altered, if it might be easily done." Pope made the alteration, on this advice, with a new word for "aching," though his "pensive bosoms" seems no real improvement.

In all poetry Swift was conscious of phonetic effects and the relation of meter to meaning. In his "Description of a City Shower," to choose from a familiar poem, the jerky, repeated *i*'s in the excellent line "BrIsk Susan whIps her lInen from the rope" suggest the hurried action of clothes being snatched from a clothesline. And in his satirical "Directions for a Birth-day Song" he advises court-poets that "Hard, tough cramp, gutt'rall, harsh, stiff names" like Hesse Darmstadt and Guelph are unsuited to adulatory verse, whereas the name "Caroline" is itself a kind of music. Though his purpose is chiefly satirical, his rhymed analysis of the phonetics in "Caroline" shows his consciousness of the subject:

> Three syllables did never meet
> So soft, so sliding, and so sweet.
> Nine other tuneful words like that
> Would prove ev'n Homer's numbers flat.
> Behold three beauteous vowels stand
> With bridegroom liquids hand in hand,

> In concord here for ever fixt,
> No jarring consonant betwixt.
> (225-232)

In the turgid, early odes, alliteration, assonance, and other sound-combinations are painfully deliberate. Such a desperately versified line as "CHIEF CHERub, and CHIEF lamp of that SACred SEVen," from the ode to Dr. Sancroft, begins unmistakably with a series of sneezes. Just such an effect might have been sought in later, more mature work, but not to grace a solemn ode. Like the following excerpts, it would have suited the mood of a humorous ballad or an angry lampoon:

> Said to the PIPpin, PLUMP, and PRIM
> ("On the Words—Brother Protestant," 13)

> Not BEGgar's BRAT, on BULK BEgot
> ("On Poetry: A Rapsody," 33)

> They CUDGell'd, and CUFT him, and KICKT him down stairs
> ("The True English Dean to Be Hanged for a Rape," 16)

> All their MADness MAKES ME MERry
> ("Epistle to a Lady," 164)

> Like a BEAU in the BOX, he BOW'D low on each side
> ("Clever Tom Clinch Going to Be Hanged," 10)

> Then GLUTtony, with GREASy PAWS,
> Her napkin PINN'D up to her jaws,
> WITH WATry CHAPS, and WAGging CHIN
> ("A Panegyrick on the Dean," 255-257)

> I MURder poor MILton
> ("My Lady's Lamentation," 156)

> SIT STILL, and SWALlow down your SPITtle
> ("On Poetry: A Rapsody," 122)

Swift's versification is not always so eager to show the tricks it can do. The contemplative lines of "Verses on the Death of Dr. Swift" do not often hiss like "Sit still and swallow down your spittle." In the glowing lines of the verses to Stella there are combinations of sound and rhythm that occasionally seem almost like Donne's or Marvell's. When he is

not trying to scarify, Swift's couplets—out of their context—
can be as deceptively simple as Mother Goose rhymes or
little songs by Herrick, or as smooth as expert limericks:

> Through candle-light she view'd the wine,
> To see that ev'ry glass was fine.
> > ("Stella at Wood-Park," 19-20)

> To cry the bread was stale, and mutter
> Complaints against the royal butter.
> > . . .
> Whilst Lady Charlotte, like a stroller,
> Sits mounted on the garden roller.
> > ("Richmond-Lodge and Marble-Hill,"
> > > 53-54, 61-62)

> Last night was so extremely fine,
> The ladies walk'd till after nine.
> > ("Cadenus and Vanessa," 326-327)

If these charming couplets were to be printed without iden-
tification, even the admirers of Swift would probably not name
him at once as the author. By persons supposed to have read
him, Jonathan Swift has so often been airily dismissed as a
versifier limited to octosyllabic jingles on angry or uncom-
fortable subjects, that it is important to make a point of the
variety in his poetry. Variety is there—in his odes, heroic
couplets, quatrains, ballads, adaptations and translations
from Latin, *vers d'occasion*, parodies, narratives, street ven-
dors' cries, riddles, and experiments with rhyme and length
of line. It was characteristic of him in both his poetry and
prose to experiment, mimic, assume a foreign style, and write
under pretense of not being Swift.

He could write headlong, ragged doggerel like that of John
Skelton two centuries earlier:

> Hail fellow, well met,
> All dirty and wet:
> Find out, if you can,
> Whose master, whose man;
> Who makes the best figure,
> The Dean or the digger;

And which is the best
At cracking a jest.
      ("My Lady's Lamentation," 165-172)

Or he could pretend to a style almost Shakespearean:

In dagger-contests, and th' artillery of words,
(For swords are madmen's tongues, and tongues are
                              madmen's swords)...
      ("Ode to Dr. William Sancroft," 13-14)

   Still a third fragment, written in his sixty-sixth year, does
not have the sound of any other poetry by him:

I walk before no man, a hawk in his fist,
Nor am I a brilliant, whenever I list.

Here is his favorite pattern of four stresses, but in a long
line; an uncharacteristic sharply-marked caesura divides the
lines; and the curiously obscure imagery might be Romantic,
perhaps modern. The imagery might well be obscure, as much
so as that in *Kubla Khan:* for, like a proper Romantic poet,
Swift dreamed the couplet. Under two illegible lines on the
blank page of a book, he wrote—in delectable mock-serious-
ness: "I waked at two this morning with the two above lines
in my head, which I had made in my sleep, and I wrote them
down in the dark, lest I should forget them. But as the original words being writ in the dark, may possibly be mistaken
by a careless or unskilful transcriber, I shall give a fairer
copy, that two such precious lines may not be lost to posterity."
   Overshadowing all this diversity, however, is Swift's almost
constant mood of parody in his poetry. And, of course, the
great preponderance of it is written in octosyllabic couplets.
It was this verse-form that Pope naturally appropriated for
his "Seventh Epistle of the First Book of Horace, Imitated
in the Manner of Dr. Swift" and that Goldsmith used for his
"New Simile, in the Manner of Swift." The octosyllabic iambic
couplet, which Samuel Butler passed along to Swift. is admirably suited to humorous or satiric verse. It is not encumbered
by length, and half of its syllables carry a stress of voice, so

that it can rattle, sputter, snicker, and curse in a way unattained in longer, more dignified, and more elegant lines. But because it can reproduce the sound of natural, simple speech and song, it has been used not only for satire and imprecation, but for some of the loveliest lyrics of Lodge, Jonson, Herrick, Lovelace, and Marvell.

In Samuel Butler's hands this four-stress verse had irregularity but little variety. And his two- and three-syllable rhymes, like "laden"/"Madam," "at a rate"/"adequate," and "sisters"/"whiskers," were deliberately crude. Swift borrowed multi-syllabic rhyming for his lampoons and trifles, but his accent, as in "bitter at" / "illiterate," usually falls where it would in normal speech. A comparison of his style with that of Butler will show how he improved upon his borrowings:

From Butler's HUDIBRAS

> But no beast ever was so slight
> For Man, as for his God, to fight.
> They have more wit, alas! and know
> Themselves and us better than so.
> But we, we onely do infuse
> The rage in them like *boute-feus.*
> 'Tis our example that instills
> In them th' infection of our ills.
> For as some late philosophers
> Have well observed, beasts that converse
> With Man, take after him, as hogs
> Get pigs all th' year, and bitches dogs.
>   (I, 775-786)

From Swift's BEASTS CONFESSION

> Creatures of ev'ry kind but ours
> Well comprehend their nat'ral pow'rs;
> While we, whom *reason* ought to sway,
> Mistake our talents ev'ry day:
> The ass was never known so stupid
> To act the part of Tray, or Cupid;

> Nor leaps upon his master's lap,
> There to be stroak'd and fed with pap;
> As Aesop would the world perswade;
> He better understands his trade:
> Nor comes, whene'er his lady whistles;
> But, carries loads, and feeds on thistles.
>
> (203-214)

The four-stress verse for Swift is sometimes brisk and hard-riding, sometimes flexible and swirling, and sometimes cold and plain. It most often shows itself in iambic couplets. But it appears in quatrains for "The Progress of Beauty"; in triplets, which he elsewhere deplored, for verses "To the Earl of Peterborow"; and in alternation with three-stress lines for "Advice to the Grub-Street Verse Writers." In "The Grand Question Debated" the four stresses are spread out among anapests; and in "The Legion Club," in which the intention is vilification and violence, the line begins with a stress, like the sound of a whip striking a table.

Byron once wrote enviously that Swift "beats us all hollow, his rhymes are wonderful." In *Don Juan*—notorious for its un-expected rhymes—Byron is indeed seldom more inventive than Swift in such a poem as "Directions for a Birth-day Song," with its "ferks his"/"Xerxes," "spoke all"/"local," "tri-dent"/"ride in't," and "Willy put"/"Lilliput." Even though he always tipped his verse with rhyme, sometimes disyllabic or trisyllabic, Swift did not see an enemy in unrhymed poetry. "As to your blank verse," he advised a correspondent, "it has too often fallen into... vile hands of late. One Thomson, a Scotchman, has succeeded the best in that way, in four poems he has writ on the four seasons, yet I am not overfond of them, because they are all description, and nothing is do-ing, whereas Milton engages me in actions of the highest im-portance..." Swift's objection to *The Seasons* is not based on any aversion to blank verse.

But he did object impatiently to rhymes that offended his ear. When he wrote to Pope about the translation of Homer, it was to express annoyance "at some bad rhymes and trip-lets..." And in his copy of Dr. James Gibbs's paraphrase of the Psalms, he scribbled disdainful comments alongside tone-deaf rhymes like "pride"/"destroy'd" and "more"/"pow'r." For the first he wrote, "Pronounce it like the Scotch," and for the second, "Pronounce this like my lady's woman."

Though it had less foundation than his dislike for ugly, inexact rhyme, his hatred for triple rhyme was almost an obsession. Perhaps, as Lord Orrery believed, there was an exterior reason for Swift's hatred—a reason bound up in personalities and not in mere versification. It occurred to Orrery that it was not so much a matter of prejudice against the practice itself, as against certain poets: "Mr. Dryden," he noted, "abounds in triplets..." and "Mr. Waller...generally reserved the nicest point of wit to his triplicate line..."

Something must now be said about diction, though Herbert Davis's excellent analysis of the diction in Swift's prose applies equally well to the poetry. As Mr. Davis makes clear, Swift was characteristically concise in all his writings, with a conciseness that has defied imitation.

Swift's diction in his poems seems for the most part intended to be spoken and conversational rather than sung or declaimed. For a poet like Chaucer this speaking voice is almost tender; for Swift it is generally witty, occasionally didactic, and now and then indignant. Unless it is assisting in parody, the vocabulary is natural and easy. Though Dr. Johnson professed indifference to the poetry, he and his assistants set down samples of it on almost every page of his Dictionary to show the use of "charms" and "chatter," "decorum," "glibber," "goody," "gracefulness," "ironically," "night-cap," "poetical," "satirick," "spittle," and words equally various. "Blab," "huddle," "jerk," "jog," "jug," "waddle," and "wag," however inelegant they may be, are not too easy-going for poetry: in Dr. Johnson's Dictionary Swift shares the authority for their use with Shakespeare and Milton. Swift's dictum of "proper words in proper places" did not exclude "clitter-clatter," "hoddy-doddy," "ninny," "noddle," and "tattle" from his poetry.

In the verses called "Apollo's Edict" Swift pokes fun at tired-out phrases like "lips of coral," "teeth of pearl,"

"deep yet clear," and "halcyon days," that are still in the
running after two hundred years. When he appropriated such
clichés for his own poetry, it was generally with parody in
mind. He did not believe in pretending to find virtues in the
dead diction of an obscure, uninspired poem. He knew what
to do with it, as he demonstrates brilliantly in his verses
"On Burning a Dull Poem":

> The cold conceits, the chilling thoughts,
> Went down like stupifying draughts:
> I found my head began to swim,
> A numbness crept through ev'ry limb:
> In haste, with imprecations dire,
> I threw the volume in the fire:
> When, who could think, tho' cold as ice,
> It burnt to ashes in a trice.
>
> How could I more enhance its fame?
> Though born in snow, it dy'd in flame.
>   (7-16)

It would be strange if there were no images, allegories,
metaphors, puns, and symbols in the poetry of Jonathan Swift;
for they are brilliant in his prose, as the following verbal
feats, the first from *A Tale of a Tub* and the second from
Gulliver's Travels, can demonstrate:

> Is not religion a cloak, honesty a pair of shoes, worn out
> in the dirt, self-love a surtout, vanity a shirt, and con-
> science a pair of breeches?

> For instance, they can decypher a close-stool to signify
> a privy-council; a flock of geese, a senate; a lame dog,
> an invader; the plague, a standing army; a buzzard, a min-
> ister; the gout, a high priest; a gibbet, a secretary of
> state; a chamber pot, a committee of grandees; a sieve,
> a court lady; a broom, a revolution; a mouse-trap, an em-
> ployment; a bottomless pit, the treasury; a sink, a court;
> a cap and bells, a favourite; a broken reed, a court of
> justice; an empty tun, a general; a running sore, the ad-
> ministration.

As they stand, these two lists of symbols have the appearance
of notes for poems on religion and the state. The first, indeed,
might be read like this:

> Is not religion a cloak,
> Honesty a pair of shoes,
> Worn out in the dirt,
> Self-love a surtout,
> Vanity a shirt,
> And conscience a pair of breeches?

Comparison, either explicit or vague, is one of the bases
for all poetry; but when Swift builds upon a simile it is, rather
than a lovely woman's resemblance to a sweet-scented rose
or a teardrop's resemblance to a little world, apt to be one of
intentionally un-"poetic" irony, paradox, and wit. The innocent reader who thinks of poetry as a silken grab-bag of metaphors from which posies, bonbons, and silver do-dads may be
drawn, is likely to reach into a poem by Swift and draw out a
spitball or a tarantula. Classical embellishments, for example,
when they appear in his poetry, are often surprisingly introduced:

> Ovid had warn'd her to beware,
>   Of stroling gods, whose usual trade is,
> Under pretence of taking air,
>   To pick up sublunary ladies.
>   ("Apollo Outwitted," 21-24)

> Here poor Pomona sits on thorns:
> And there neglected Flora settles
> Her bum upon a bed of nettles.
>   ("The Dean's Reasons," 92-94)

> There Cerberus lay watching in his den,
> (He had not seen a hare the Lord knows when)...
>   ("On Mr. Pulteney," 25-26)

> When first Diana leaves her bed
> Vapors and steams her looks disgrace,
> A frouzy dirty colour'd red
> Sits on her cloudy wrinckled face...
>   ("The Progress of Beauty," 1-4)

In the absurd or rude context Ovid's gods, Pomona and Flora, Cerberus, and Diana are divested of their classical dignity in order to create a new relationship and meaning.

When Swift uses this device in reverse, it is to turn a dignified subject into satire, to singe a pompous dunce, or to scorch a political enemy. "The Progress of Poetry," a sober subject in other writers' hands, is built upon the analogy between a prosperous poet and a goose that has grown too fat to fly and sing. "On Poetry: A Rapsody" compares a hard-labored poem to the chicken that requires a month to fatten but is devoured and forgotten in a few minutes. In other poems intended to vex, instruct, or amuse, the barnyard contributes still further similes in a frustrated hen, a flooded stable, a skinny cow, and a larva in a meal-bin. Most famous of all in the poetry are the ass, swine, and goat of "The Beasts Confession."

Whatever else he may be, Swift is not a rural or "folksy" writer. Instead, as in Chaucer's story of Chauntecleer and Dame Pertelote, who discuss Boethius in the henhouse, there is almost a sophistication in the rude buffeting of anti-"sublime" barnyard associations in a new context. Perhaps he leads chickens, cows, horses, and pigs into his verse in order to laugh at the growing literature concerned with the Happy Beast. Poets like Thomson and Pope had joined Locke to say that animals have powers of reason, opposing other poets like Young who held to Descartes' conception of animals as mere automata. In depicting men as crass, unreasoning Yahoos and animals as noble Houyhnhnms, Swift turns the whole argument into absurdity. His "Beasts Confession," pushing the Lockean theory to its wildest extreme, concludes with the casual observation that

> now and then
> Beasts may *degen'rate* into men.
> (219-220)

Le mythe animal for Swift is almost never a matter of antelopes, unicorns, tigers, and fabulous giraffes popular in medieval "bestiaries." One of the most memorable passages in *The Battle of the Books* is that which likens a certain kind

of wit to skimmed milk for the hogs. Elsewhere in his prose
the best example of this effect is in the delineation of the
Houyhnhnms, also drawn from the barnyard, but elevated
above it and even above the barnyard that is called polite
civilization.

It will be remembered that those admirable horses, the
Houyhnhnms, represent Swift's idea of reasonable, uncor-
rupted goodness in poetry, as in every endeavor of life. Like
Swift himself, the Houyhnhnms express themselves with
"justness" and "exactness." They are, however, ideal
creatures and create ideal poetry that is probably not very
lively. For unlike Swift the Houyhnhnms are not blessed by
humor and the sin of wit: "In poetry they must be allowed to
excel all other mortals; wherein the justness of their similes,
and the minuteness, as well as the exactness of their descriptions, are indeed inimitable."

CHAPTER TWO

HUMOUR, AND MIRTH, HAD PLACE IN ALL HE WRIT

1.

SWIFT'S IDEA OF HUMOR

"I have observed," Lord Bathurst wrote to Jonathan Swift on April 19, 1731, "that in comedy, the best actor plays the part of a droll, while some scrub rogue is made the hero, or fine gentleman. So, in this farce of life, wise men pass their time in mirth, while fools only are serious. Adieu. Continue to be merry and wise; but never turn serious, or cunning."

On this letter Swift superscribed the words: "It is too late for me to turn serious now."

It was too late for him to strike humor and mirth from *The Battle of the Books, A Tale of a Tub, The Drapier's Letters, Gulliver's Travels,* and the *Miscellanies;* too late for him to make them the wholly grave and didactic works they might have been. He was, in 1731, writing of his own death in a humorous vein, commenting on envy, friendship, the life of Man, and his own situation in verses that are a masterly elaboration of the theme, "It is too late for me to turn serious now."

Swift's idea of humor remained little changed throughout his life, and on several occasions, in verse and prose, he set down definitions, differentiating humor from its sister, wit. The Author's Apology for *A Tale of a Tub* concludes with the observation that humor is the "most agreeable" gift of human nature. More than thirty years later almost the same phrases appear in the Irish *Intelligencer*, No. III, 1728: "...humour, which in its perfection is allowed to be much preferable to wit, if it be not rather the most useful, and agreeable species of it..." Under the title of "A Vindication of Mr. Gay, and the Beggar's Opera" this essay from the *Intelligencer* is a defense of that talent so delightful to most persons but described as "low" by contemptuous grim critics. The "low" humor or comedy exalted by Rabelais in France, Cervantes in Spain, and "those volumes printed in France, under the name of Le Theatre Italien," Swift says, is a happy talent natural to even the simplest schoolboy or apprentice. Though the schoolboy is not, and will very probably never be, a good judge of poetry, eloquence, and music, he knows almost infallibly whether a thing is funny or not; and the apprentice requires neither special cultivation of taste nor any Aristotelian measuring rod to feel instinctively that he must slap his thigh and bellow with laughter, lie on the floor and kick with joy, or, the humor failing, draw a long face. On its most artistic level, in the literature of *The Beggar's Opera, Gargantua* and *Pantagruel, Don Quixote*, or the Commedia dell' Arte, laughter depends heavily upon characterization and the antics of characters who find themselves caught in a humorous situation. *The Beggar's Opera*, which Swift is ostensibly vindicating here against dull or affected critics, is a performance wherein, he says, the grotesque characters are wholly believable and move in a framework of recognizable satire. He is explicit in identifying humor with characterization and in isolating it as a natural taste that we can observe everywhere, "among common servants, and the meanest of people, while the very owners are very often ignorant of the gift they possess." He is still more explicit in verses "To Mr. Delany," 1718:

> What humor is, not all the tribe
> Of logick-mongers can describe;

Here, onely Nature acts her part,
Unhelpt by practice, books, or art.
For wit and humor differ quite,
That gives surprise, and this delight:
Humor is odd, grotesque, and wild,
Onely by affectation spoild,
Tis never by invention got,
Men have it when they know it not.
(19-28)

Though the Elizabethan "humors" of personification were going out of fashion in the eighteenth century, humor itself was a literary quality upon which the English prided themselves, calling it native to their country. For them it was conversation or characterization that was natural, familiar, individual, and delightful. Dryden, in the Epilogue to *The Wild Gallant, Revived*, 1667, called humor "that which every day we meet"; Temple's "Of Poetry," 1690, described it as "a picture of a particular life"; and Congreve, in "Concerning Humour in Comedy," 1696, wrote: "I take it to be a singular and unavoidable manner of doing or saying anything peculiar and natural to one man only, by which his speech and actions are distinguished from those of other men." Such points of view very likely helped to form Swift's idea of an odd, native humor that we express even when we "know it not." He is so often described as a tormented genius whose skepticism became madness, that it is hard to remember he liked a joke better than most geniuses and that he loved *la bagatelle*, even seeking to use laughter as a weapon of reform. It was mirth for its own sake when he wrote "A Meditation upon a Broom-Stick," rhymed "sorcery" with "horse awry," amused Stella with his "little language," devised riddles in rhyme to tease his friends, and turned the commonplace into funny verse. There is an underlying and over-all spirit of fun in Swift. When little Marjory Fleming confided to her Journal that "Doctor Swift's works are very funny & amusing & I get some by hart," she was at least as discerning as her elders to whom Swift's works seemed heartless.

2.

ACTING IN CHARACTER

What there is to grin at in Swift's poetry often arises from characterization through monologue and dialogue ingeniously adapted to rhyme. His cookmaids, noblemen, idle wives, clergymen, bookdealers, and politicians speak unmistakably in voices of their own. They ramble or superciliously condescend, gabble, or protest in turn.

We have a charming instance of Swift's ability with humorous monologue: almost as entertaining as Laetitia Pilkington's account of his running up one flight of stairs and down another for exercise, is her description of his "acting in character":

> The bottle and glasses being taken away, the Dean set about making the coffee; but the fire scorching his hand, he called to me to reach him his glove, and changing the coffee-pot to his left-hand, held out his right one, ordered me to put the glove on it, which accordingly I did; when taking up part of his gown to fan himself with, and acting in character of a prudish lady, he said, "Well, I do not know what to think; women may be honest that do such things, but, for my part, I never could bear to touch any man's flesh—except my husband's," whom perhaps, says he, she wished at the devil.

In prose dialogue Swift is best represented by his *Polite Conversation*, which like his most characteristic work in both prose and poetry is not what it purports to be. No model and handbook of witty repartee, it mercilessly records the heavy-handed jests and horseplay, the warmed-over cynicism and tattle of Persons of Quality. Miss Notable, whose retorts are immediate and brisk, is the heroine of the piece; and she has the last word. At three in the morning when the company rises from the game of quadrille, Tom Neverout chooses from among the flowers of wit and language to remark, "Faith, I'm for *Bed*fordshire," and addresses Miss Notable with his unflag-

ging insolence: "Miss, I hope you'll dream of your sweetheart." "Oh, no doubt of it," says she: "I believe I shan't
be able to sleep for dreaming of him." George Saintsbury confessed in *The Peace of the Augustans* that "One remains at
the feet of Miss Notable; and is almost ashamed to babble
about the idol."

Even with the husks of her clichés lying about her, "Miss"
charms the reader; and in rhyme Mrs. Frances Harris and Mary
the Cookmaid share her charm. Their doggerel depicts them
clearly; they might have come this morning from the company
of Fielding's Mrs. Honour, Mrs. Slipslop, and Molly Seagrim.
They are drawn so truly that nymphs and dryads, dancing in
flowery meadows, seem a plague in poetry indeed; and are not
so prepossessing as this distressed waiting-woman and indignant cookmaid. "Lord! I thought I should have sunk out-
right," "Pugh, said I," and "faith and troth!" they exclaim.
To them the household details of life are all-important: they
cannot speak without telling in specific detail how money is
kept "in my pocket ty'd about my middle, next my smock,"
or how a day is remembered because "I was mending my
master's stocking." And they name names: Lady Betty, Mrs.
Dukes, deaf Dame Wadgar, Lord Dromedary, Sister Marget,
and the Dean. Obligingly, Mrs. Harris attempts to be legally
exact in telling what sum of money she lost and what everyone said about her misfortune. Like the gentlefolk in *Polite
Conversation* they appreciate the flavor of a well-tried phrase:
"hardly ... slept a wink" and "I would not give such language to a dog..." Like all good folk they gladly throw out
moral observations that "of all things in the world, I hate a
thief," and "I am sure such words does not become a man of
your cloth." Acting in character, providing them with the
fiddle-faddle of homely detail, Swift has them speak humorously and believably.

"To Their Excellencies the Lords Justices of Ireland: The
Humble Petition of Frances Harris, Who Must Starve, and Die
a Maid if It Miscarries," 1701, was written while Swift was
chaplain to Lord Berkeley in Ireland. Mrs. Harris, one of Lady
Berkeley's waiting women, is distressed to tears over losing
her purse with its "seven pound, four shillings and six pence,

besides farthings, in money and gold":

> So next morning we told Whittle, and he fell a swearing;
> Then my Dame Wadgar came, and she, you know, is thick
>   of hearing;
> *Dame*, said I, as loud as I could bawl, do you know what
>   a loss I have had?
> Nay, said she, my Lord Collway's folks are all very sad,
> For my Lord Dromedary comes a Tuesday without fail;
> Pugh! said I, but that's not the business that I ail.
>   (24-29)

From the valet, who can only curse, to Lord Berkeley himself, all the household hears the story. But Mrs. Harris is seeking sympathy chiefly, for she has dreamed very specifically that the money is in a rag in a corner of a box belonging to Mrs. Dukes, whom she approaches on the subject. Mrs. Dukes blesses herself, roars, and denies having seen the purse, leaving poor Mrs. Harris as wise as she was before. Her discourse with her favorite, the chaplain, is even less happy, for she calls him Parson and asks whether he can "cast a Nativity, when a body's plunder'd." He is annoyed and tells her so.

> With that, he twisted his girdle at me like a rope, as who
>   should say,
> Now you may go hang your self for me, and so went away.
> Well; I thought I should have swoon'd: *Lord*, said I, what
>   shall I do?
> I have lost my money, and I shall lose my true-love too.
>   (62-65)

And so Mrs. Harris submits her petition to the Lords Justices of Ireland, one of whom is her employer, requesting "a share in next Sunday's collection..." Further, while she is making requests, she asks for conferment of orders upon the chaplain, unless, she casually adds, an even more attractive chaplain can be found:

> And then your poor petitioner, both night and day,

Or the chaplain, (for 'tis his trade) as in duty bound, shall
   ever pray.

(74-75)

Here Mrs. Harris is wonderfully parenthetical. Mary the
Cookmaid is more direct, more simple-minded, and less at
ease with a pen, more apt to blunder into garbled phrases
like "parsonable man" and "come-rogues." She was Swift's
own cook, towards the end of his life, a robust woman with a
pockmarked face and addressed by him as "Sweetheart."
"Mary the Cook-Maid's Letter to Dr. Sheridan," 1718—included in W.H. Auden's *Oxford Book of Light Verse*—is the
best known of the roguish rhymes exchanged in Swift's Irish
circle. Sheridan had been called a goose; in retaliation he
called Swift a knave; to reply, Swift acts in character to become Mary the Cookmaid, praising her master.

> He has more goodness in his little finger, than you have
>   in your whole body,
> My master is a parsonable man, and not a spindle-shank'd
>   hoddy-doddy.
>
>   . . .
>
> Every body knows, that I love to tell truth and shame the
>   the devil,
> I am but a poor servant, but I think gentle folks should be
>   civil.
> Besides, you found fault with our vittles one day that you
>   was here,
> I remember it was upon a Tuesday, of all days in the year.

(9-10, 23-26)

First of all, laughingly, Swift is using Mrs. Harris's voice
and Mary's to express something without seeming to; then
through their voices he suggests vividly their actual pre-
sences, their accusing eyes, their frowns, their fingers grasp-
ing the pen-quill; and third, he has them speak in a rambling
tattle of inventive humor, never for a syllable slipping out of
character. His ear for the wandering cadence of speech and
his eye for funny portraits worked together to create in these,
as in his other verses meant to be giggled at, an odd batch of

rhymes and rhythms.* When Thomas Hardy tried the same sort
of thing in "The Chapel Organist," "In the Servants' Quar-
ters," and other long-lined monologues and dialogues, he for
once lacked the ingenuity of Swift, of whom William Hazlitt
wrote in appreciation: "He has gone so far as to invent a new
stanza of fourteen and sixteen syllable lines for Mary the
cookmaid to vent her budget of nothings, and for Mrs. Harris
to gossip with the deaf old housekeeper." Other critics regret
that he did not more often find time for this very attractive
kind of doggerel: it proves, they say, that he did not have to
be unpleasant in what he wrote.

There is no more humor in his indulgent pretense of being
a cookmaid than there is in his pretense in rhyme of speaking
for an idle lady of fashion. But, partly because they do not
warm the heart, but rather chill it, Swift's tenser, more biting
lines, in which ladies of quality vent *their* budgets of nothing,
do not so often find admirers. A society of fashionably dressed,
charmless ladies moves noisily through Swift's writing: they
are the Lady Smart and Lady Answerall of *Polite Conversation*; the "tribe of bold, swaggering, rattling ladies" of "A
Letter to a Young Lady on her Marriage"; the Brobdingnagian
maids of honor; the silly recipient of "Verses Wrote in a
Lady's Ivory Table Book"; Phillis in "The Progress of
Love," who would "heave her bosom" in church for "beaux
to see it bare"; the gadabout wife in "The Progress of Marriage," wearing "French brocades and Flanders lace"; and
the smart lady who "calls it witty to be rude" in "The Furniture of a Woman's Mind." They talk and talk and talk; in
"The Journal of a Modern Lady," 1729, Swift describes the
din they raise:

> Now voices over voices rise;
> While each to be the loudest vies,
> They contradict, affirm, dispute,
> No single tongue one moment mute;

*Were Swift's long-lined gabbling poems inspired by the High
Church service, which also has long clauses that are gabbled
off hurriedly until they reach a rhythmical and logical pause?
I owe this ingenious suggestion to Professor Gilbert Highet.

All mad to speak, and none to hearken,
They set the very lap-dog barking;
Their chattering makes a louder din
Than fish-wives o'er a cup of gin:
Not school-boys at a barring-out,
Rais'd ever such incessant rout:
The jumbling particles of matter
In chaos made not such a clatter:
Far less the rabble roar and rail,
When drunk with sour election ale.

                              (174-187)

There is not much variety or much that scintillates in what
they have to say: they are descendants of the Earl of Rochester's indefatigable talkers in "Tunbridge Wells" and an-
cestresses of T.S. Eliot's "Doris," who drew the coffin when
she cut the cards and kept talking about it. Swift's card-playing ladies, who spend the night at quadrille, are immortally
represented by the "female friends" in the verses on his
death; in "The Journal of a Modern Lady" they are equally
indefatigable in conversation:

"This morning when the parson came,
"I said I should not win a game.
"This odious chair how came I stuck in't,
"I think I never had good luck in't.
"I'm so uneasy in my stays;
"Your fan, a moment, if you please.
"Stand further girl, or get you gone.
"I always lose when you look on.

                              (238-245)

This is, in effect, *Polite Conversation* in verse, with the de-
light of humor and recognition augmented by rhyme and rhythm.
The tone is shriller when the "glitt'ring dames" are heard in
"Cadenus and Vanessa":

Their clamour 'lighting from their chairs,
Grew louder, all the way up stairs...
                    . . .
——I'm sorry Mopsa breaks so fast;

> I said her face would never last.
> Corinna with that youthful air,
> Is thirty, a nd a bit to spare.
> Her fondness for a certain earl
> Began, when I was but a girl.
>
>   . . .
>
> They railly'd next Vanessa's dress:
> That gown was made for old Queen Bess.
> Dear Madam, let me set your head:
> Don't you intend to put on red?
>   (368-369, 386-391, 396-399)

Eighteenth-century fops with their "soft voice and speech absurd" are portrayed similarly in "Cadenus and Vanessa" and elsewhere; but when Swift acted in character, it was the "incessant rout" of fine ladies that he most outrageously mimicked.

Humorous characterization of poets, parsons, statesmen, lawyers, and soldiers is fitted to the pattern of monologue and dialogue in many of Swift's verses. In "Richmond-Lodge and Marble-Hill," 1727, there is even a pastoral dialogue between two houses in the manner of Thomas Hardy's "The Two Houses," "The Aged Newspaper Soliloquizes," and "Haunting Fingers," in which musical instruments talk in the night. Swift's rhyme s on poets and parsons were often autobiographical; but he wrote witL distrust and dislike of statesmen in many verses, best perhaps in "Ireland," from the "Holyhead Journal," 1727; of lawyers in "The Answer to 'Paulus'," 1728; and of soldiers in "The Grand Question Debated," 1729. All are described, with an intensity that excludes humor, in an imitation of Petronius, "On Dreams," 1724:

> The statesman rakes the town to find a plot,
> And dreams of forfeitures by treason got.
>
>   . . .
>
> Orphans around his bed the lawyer sees,
> And takes the plaintiff's and defendant's fees.
>
>   . . .
>
> The soldier smiling hears the widows' cries,
> And stabs the son before the mother's eyes.
>   (19-20, 23-24, 15-16)

In "The Grand Question Debated," sometimes called "A
Soldier and a Scholar," there is delightful characterization of
a captain as he is imagined by a lady's maid: we first watch
his arrival and then share his conversation at dinner:

> See, now comes the Captain all dawb'd with gold lace:
> Oh law! the sweet gentleman! look in his face;
> And see how he rides like a lord of the land,
> With the fine flaming sword that he holds in his hand...
>   . . .
> "To give a young gentleman right education,
> "The Army's the only good school in the nation;
> "My school-master call'd me a dunce and a fool,
> "But at cuffs I was always the cock of the school;
> "I never cou'd take to my book for the blood o'me,
> "And the puppy confess'd, he expected no good o'me.
> "He caught me one morning coquetting his wife,
> "But he maul'd me, I ne'er was so maul'd in my life;
> "So, I took to the road, and what's very odd,
> "The first man I robb'd was a parson by G—.
> "Now Madam, you'll think it a strange thing to say,
> "But, the sight of a book makes me sick to this day.
>   (93-96, 161-172)

Read alongside the breathless gabble of fashionable ladies,
this captain's gross, deliberate, egotistic monologue seems
an admirable example of Swift's acting in character. It is
bright humor from a cynic and misanthrope who knew that it
was too late for him to turn serious.

3.

VANESSA, STELLA, AND DAPHNE

Swift's humorous characterization of personal relationships
may best be seen in verses addressed to three women: "Vanessa," "Stella," and "Daphne." When Swift wrote with
tenderness and affection he wrote, as an honest poet should,
most warily of the artificial phrase, the false-sounding note,
and the extravagance that rings of insincerity. Because roman-

tic, passionate ecstasy seemed to him a subject for burlesque, his own tender sentiments were usually expressed quietly in humorous understatement or hidden in raillery. Much of the interest in his affectionate verses, therefore, lies in seeing how expertly he wrote within the constraining bounds he set for himself.

Perhaps because it seems almost conventionally tender, "Cadenus and Vanessa," 1713, the longest of all the poems and least characteristic of the important ones, has sometimes been considered the height of Swift's accomplishment in rhyme. When Goldsmith described it as one of the author's correctest pieces, he explained its good reception; for though the subject matter itself is somewhat odd, the treatment is fashionable and elegantly formal with a glossy film of urbanity meant to flatter the romantic girl for whom the poem was written. Esther Vanhomrigh, according to Dr. Johnson, was "a woman made unhappy by her admiration of wit, and ignominiously distinguished by the name of Vanessa... She was a young woman fond of literature, whom Decanus the Dean, called Cadenus by transposition of the letters, took pleasure in directing and instructing; till, from being proud of his praise, she grew fond of his person." This is the substance of the poem itself, in which Swift has the girl finally undertake to instruct her teacher in matters of love, though with what success the reader is coyly kept from learning. Within its elaborate framework of goddesses, cupids, shepherds, harnessed doves, and long pleas heard by the Queen of Love, Vanessa's little story is almost lost in the paper lace of an unwieldy valentine. Because the talent of Swift lay rather in the composition of comic valentines touched with genius—more like Michelangelo's cartoons than the fêtes champêtres of Watteau—this poem seems written in a borrowed language at which Swift usually laughed. It is not mock- but pseudo-classical. Herbert Davis has noted that on another occasion, perhaps in the same year, Swift wrote a briefer poem in the same vein: the chaste goddesses and ravished youths of the verses "To Lord Harley, on his Marriage" are also pseudo-classical in spirit.

The opening lines of "Cadenus and Vanessa" remind the

reader of fanciful songs by an elegant and tiresome poet like
the Countess of Winchilsea:

> The shepherds and the nymphs were seen
> Pleading before the Cyprian Queen.
> The council for the fair began,
> Accusing that false creature, Man.
>
> (1-4)

The case being pleaded is to determine whether men or women
are more responsible for the faults of modern love (1-125);
Judge Venus, calling a recess, experiments with a "wondrous"
nymph, Vanessa, who is endowed with male virtues (126-303);
but Vanessa does not attract suitors and is herself disdainful
of society, preferring to read Montaigne (304-464); Cupid fixes
her affection upon her tutor, Cadenus (465-827); and when the
law case is resumed, Venus's decree is against the men, who
were too tasteless to appreciate Vanessa (828-889).

Andreas Capellanus's account of medieval Courts of Love,
adapted to suit the Age of Reason, if such a thing can be
imagined, would probably resemble this poem. Much of its
humor comes from the intrusion of worldly things into a celes-
tial scene, as when the verses of Cowley and Waller are con-
sulted for authority in Heaven. The disparity in age between
the young Vanessa and her somewhat cynical old tutor lends
further amusement. But when he describes the proper educa-
tion for a sensible young woman in a world of fops and quadrille, Swift's intention is more serious. Except for a discourse
on "modern love" in lines 21-66 the first characteristically
Swiftian passage is that in which Venus praises Vanessa, the
model girl:

> Offending daughters oft would hear
> Vanessa's praise rung in their ear:
> Miss Betty, when she does a fault,
> Lets fall her knife, or spills the salt,
> Will then be by her mother chid,
> " 'Tis what Vanessa never did.
>
> (240-245)

In its courtly setting this homely detail did not please Taine, for the very reason that it is characteristic of Swift: "Singulière façon d'admirer Vanessa et de lui prouver qu'on l'admire! Je l'appelle nymphe et la traite en écolière." But in these octosyllabic couplets Swift excels, just as Chaucer excels in the octosyllabic couplets of even so allegorical a poem as "The House of Fame," when he is most original, humorous, homely, and explicit. When "Cadenus and Vanessa" is at its best, in the fashionable fops' "tattle of the day" and the ladies' "usual chat," it resembles the verses on Swift's death, and is very good indeed.

The poem was probably given to Vanessa in 1713, went from hand to hand, caused scandalized whispers, and was in 1726 published without Swift's consent, causing him some embarrassment because of what it revealed. Still more would have been revealed in complementary verses he suggested to Vanessa in 1720:

> There would be the chapter of Madam going to Kensington; the chapter of the blister; the chapter of the Colonel going to France; the chapter of the wedding, with the adventures of the lost key; of the sham; of the joyful return; two hundred chapters of madness; the chapter of long walks; the Berkshire surprise; fifty chapters of little times; the chapter of Chelsea; the chapter of swallow and cluster; a hundred whole books of myself, etc.; the chapter of hide and whisper; the chapter of who made it so; my sister's money.

These tantalizing chapters were never written, and by 1723, when Vanessa died, she had broken with Swift entirely, and he was sorry he had written "Cadenus and Vanessa": "It was," he wrote in the year it was first published, "a task performed in a frolic among some ladies."

He would not have dismissed so summarily the poems to Stella, usually addressed to her year by year on her birthdays. They contain his most gravely musical, most affecting phrases. When, in 1726, he received news of her serious illness, he wrote, almost out of control of his emotions, to James Stopford: "Dear Jim, pardon me, I know not what I am saying; but believe me that violent friendship is much more lasting, and as much engaging, as violent love." But in his poems to Stella, Swift always knew what he was saying and was never violent, no matter how great his devotion or how warm the regard he expressed. In one of the poems he reminded her that he had never sung of "Cupid's darts," "killing eyes," and "bleeding hearts," but that he had been honest and truthful in his praise of her as his friend. "Truth," he told her, "shines the brighter, clad in verse." It does shine bright in delightful verses like those "To Stella, Visiting Me in My Sickness," 1720:

> For Stella never learn'd the art,
> At proper times to scream and start;
> Nor calls up all the house at night,
> And swears she saw a thing in white.
> Doll never flies to cut her lace,
> Or throw cold water in her face,
> Because she heard a sudden drum,
> Or found an earwig in a plum.
>   (71-78)

Like phrases from Shakespearean song, the last couplet here combines rich sound and an impression of bright detail. The beat of "hearD a suDDen Drum" is as capably handled as are the blunted vowels that follow in "OR FOUND an EARwig in a PLUM." These two unpretentious lines are hardly inferior to those by Herrick that Edith Sitwell singles out to praise for their beauty, remarking on the artful effect of repeated s's, echoes, and fruit-shapes in the names "pear" and "plum":

> So silently they one to th' other come,
> As colours steal into the pear or plum.
>   (Herrick, "Lovers: How They
>   Come and Part," 5-6)

There would be loss of melody, certainly, if Herrick had written, in Swift's brisker, shorter lines, something like this:

> So silent they together come
> As colours steal in pear or plum.

But there would be only a stuffing of syllables and loss of directness if Swift, in his poem to Stella, had used Herrick's length of line:

> Because she heard a sudden sound of drum,
> Or found an earwig in a bitten plum.

The six lines next quoted, from the same poem to Stella, beginning with "When on my sickly couch I lay," seem as musical as the six from Wordsworth beginning "For oft, when on my couch I lie." Still writing with honesty joined to feeling, and without recourse to song-book language, Swift attains a quality of music in what he says:

> When on my sickly couch I lay,
> Impatient both of night and day,
> Lamenting in unmanly strains,
> Call'd ev'ry pow'r to ease my pains,
> Then Stella ran to my relief
> With chearful face, and inward grief...
> (97-102)

These lines move with continuous sound; but in lines that follow, the couplets are closed with barriers that require suspension of the voice. The quiet phrases of "Now, with a soft and silent tread" are especially slow because of substitution of a stress, "Now," and the pause that accompanies it:

> My sinking spirits now supplies
> With cordials in her hands, and eyes.
> Now, with a soft and silent tread,
> Unheard she moves about my bed.
> I see her taste each nauseous draught,
> And so obligingly am caught:
> I bless the hand from whence they came,
> Nor dare distort my face for shame.
> (109-116)

There is stronger praise in the poem, but it is no more lyrical than in these lines with their undercurrent of emotion. But however passionate or serious he may feel, there is still in Swift a wonderful sense of the absurd, as in the very gentle, wry couplet last quoted.

Sometimes, in these poems to Stella, Swift is gracefully complimentary, saying for instance, in "Stella's Birthday, March 13, 1719," that if it pleased the gods to split her into two women as lovely as she, he would beg that his worship for her might also be divided. This courtly conceit seems honest and convincing in part because the poem opens with deliberately flat, humorously unromantic lines:

> Stella this day is thirty-four,
> (We shan't dispute a year or more)...

Again, humorously, he compares her to the Angel Inn, so attractive and virtuous that it is popular even when it grows old and its sign needs paint; like Stella's, it is an "angel's face, a little crack'd." Or, when she is to go to the country for her health, he compares her to a famished cow that, sent to graze, becomes plump and vigorous again. There is an affectionate, humorous concern that lends to these poems a warmth and melody. These are qualities that can be felt and heard even in the pleasant little tribute "To Stella, Who Collected and Transcribed His Poems," 1720:

> As when a lofty pile is rais'd,
> We never hear the workmen prais'd,
> Who bring the lime, or place the stones;
> But all admire Inigo Jones:
> So if this pile of scatter'd rhymes
> Should be approv'd in after-times,
> If it both pleases and endures,
> The merit and the praise are yours.
> (1-8)

Of all these poems the last, "Stella's Birthday, March 13, 1727," written less than a year before her death, best represents Swift's own reserved kind of love-verse in which he incorporated wit, tenderness, grace, and neatness as Andrew Marvell, for instance, did at his best:

> This day, whate'er the fates decree,
> Shall still be kept with joy by me:

> This day then, let us not be told,
> That you are sick, and I grown old,
> Nor think on our approaching ills,
> And talk of spectacles and pills;
> To morrow will be time enough
> To hear such mortifying stuff.
>   (1-8)

Indeed, "To morrow will be Time enough / To hear such mort-
ifying Stuff" could without alteration conceivably have come
from the side of Marvell's "Had we but World enough, and
Time." Like Marvell, Swift can here be praised for ingenuity,
exactness, and glib freshness of phrase. There is no amusement from a blunt reminder of Stella's age or from a far-fetched
comparison to an undernourished cow; but the effect is more
certain when spectacles and pills are transformed into symbols (in the manner of the Mirror, Clock, and Smile of W.H.
Auden) for Swift's increasing years and Stella's infirmities.
Harold Williams was perhaps thinking especially of those
lines when he described the poem as "tender and beautiful."
With its "Me, surely me" the conclusion brings a note extremely personal and hardly "Swiftian":

> O then, whatever Heav'n intends,
> Take pity on your pitying friends;
> Nor let your ills affect your mind,
> To fancy they can be unkind.
> Me, surely me, you ought to spare,
> Who gladly would your suff'rings share;
> Or give my scrap of life to you,
> And think it far beneath your due;
> You, to whose care so oft I owe,
> That I'm alive to tell you so.
>   (79-88)

Throughout the years of their relationship Swift wished
Stella to be admired not so much for her beauty, or even for
her devotion, as for her independence and wit. For the very
reason that he loved her, he wilfully circumscribed her free-
dom and kept a jealous guard upon her mind. But he never-

theless imagined her as the New Woman of the middle class, like Jane Austen later in the century, whose wit could support her in conversation with the most learned or elegant gentlemen. The poems to Stella are the only sort that could conceivably have been addressed to such a woman as Jane Austen. Any man with temerity to proffer affectionate rhymes to the author of *Emma* would have made certain that they were first of all humorous, witty, and wise.

Of a very different sort are the many humorous poems Swift wrote for "Daphne," Lady Acheson, during his long visits at Market Hill, near Armagh, in the north of Ireland in 1728, 1729, and 1730. He had known her father, the Right Hon. Philip Savage, and now made himself disconcertingly at home with her and her husband, Sir Arthur, who was high sheriff for his county. Swift rearranged their gardens, punished their servants, corrected Lady Acheson, and came down to dinner only when he pleased. After his eight-months-long first visit he wrote to Pope of his entertainment in the country, where, he said, he was tutor to his "perfectly well bred" hostess and wrote "family verses of mirth by way of libels on my Lady." They were libels composed of banter, pleasantry stuck through with satire, and the humorous raillery he had commended in his poem "To Mr. Delany." Conversation at its best, he had said, combines wit and humor to create the raillery in which the French excel; it was Voiture, he pointed out, who turned irony into praise and "first found out the rule / For an obliging ridicule." Libels and "obliging ridicule" provided an evening's entertainment for Lady Acheson, her husband, and their guests: it was an honor to be insulted by the Dean.

In "The Journal of a Modern Lady," 1729, he wickedly describes the annals of a day in Lady Acheson's life: how she is awakened at noon to be reminded of last night's losses at quadrille; takes her tea and cream; is almost dressed by four; bores the dinner-guests with her stale conversation; gossips over the evening tea; and plays quadrille again, pausing only to gobble supper, until the watchman cries: "A frosty morn—past four a-clock." The card-playing ladies leave at last, and their hostess,

> With empty purse, and aching head,

> Steals to her sleeping spouse to bed.
> (292-293)

Those verses are a museum in which details of eighteenth-century upper-class life are preserved; and they are humorous verses even when they are least kindly. Later, when Swift had broken his friendship with Sir Arthur and Lady Acheson, he wrote of her in prose that has no humor: "She is an absolute Dublin rake, sits up late, loses her money, and goes to bed sick." While he was still her friend, the Dean of St. Patrick's could banter; no longer her friend, he was stern and censorious.

The vivacious verses of "My Lady's Lamentation," 1728, are even more personal than those of the "Journal"; Swift makes Lady Acheson describe herself grotesquely in lines almost Skeltonic:

> From shoulder to flank
> I'm lean and am lank;
> My nose, long and thin,
> Grows down to my chin;
> My chin will not stay,
> But meets it half way;
> My fingers, prolix,
> Are ten crooked sticks...
>
>   . . .
>
> When my elbows he sees
> Held up by my knees,
> My arms, like two props,
> Supporting my chops,
> And just as I handle 'em
> Moving all like a pendulum;
> He trips up my props,
> And down my chin drops,
> From my head to my heels,
> Like a clock without wheels;
> I sink in the spleen,
> An useless machine.
> (71-78, 25-36)

Phrases swing back and forth like a skeleton on a string until
the rhythm is broken by added syllables in "handle 'em" and
"pendulum," and everything clatters down in a heap, its motion spent.

Most humorously imaginative of the "comic valentines" for
Lady Acheson is "Death and Daphne, To an Agreeable Young
Lady, but Extremely Lean," 1730, a fable that tells how
Death wishes to mate with Daphne, who herself, somewhat
startlingly, makes the first advance; and how Death hastens
to leave her when he finds her more deathlike than he:

> Pluto observing, since the Peace,
> The burial article decrease;
> And, vext to see affairs miscarry,
> Declar'd in council, Death must marry:
> Vow'd, he no longer could support
> Old batchelors about his court...
>
>   . . .
>
> She, as he came into the room,
> Thought him Adonis in his bloom.
> And now her heart with pleasure jumps,
> She scarce remembers what is trumps.
> For, such a shape of skin and bone
> Was never seen, except her own...
>
>   (7-12, 57-62)

When Death places his finger on Daphne's dry, cold hand, the
"frighted spectre"'s thoughts of marriage freeze. The lady
Swift elsewhere called "perfectly well bred" is here, for the
fun of it, the subject of macabre insult in language of burlesque. Unlike Wordsworth's, whose "heart with pleasure
fills" or poetically "leaps up," Daphne's foolish "heart with
pleasure jumps," as though it were a nervous rabbit.

Even though the chiding poem called "Daphne," 1730, had
previously been included under the heading of Market Hill, it
was not until Williams's edition of the poems that the "extremely lean" heroine of "Death and Daphne" was identified
in print as Lady Acheson. Until then, Daphne was unaccount-
ably supposed to be the sensation-loving Mrs. Pilkington,
whose portrait by Hone shows a pretty charmer, bosomy and

far from lean. In his *Remarks* Lord Orrery does not name her,
but tells how he once heard "Death and Daphne" read, in
Swift's presence, by the lady in question. Unable to appreciate
its raillery, he could not believe the poem pleased her as
much as she insisted, until Swift "burst into a fit of laughter.
'You fancy,' says he, 'that you are very polite, but you are
much mistaken. That lady had rather be a Daphne drawn by
me, than a Sacharissa by any other pencil.'" Still incredulous,
but falling in with the game, Orrery says he whispered to the
lady to flatter her, when he took her hand, that it was indeed
"as dry and cold as lead" as the poem describes. Orrery's
annotation in his copy of the *Remarks*, now in the library of
Harvard University, does identify Daphne: alongside his account of her, he has written: "Lady Atchison, wife of Sir
Arthur Atchison. Separated from her husband." Accepting this
notation as authority for what now seems obvious, Williams
places the poem among all the other "family verses of mirth"
from Market Hill.

Sometimes, understandably, Lady Acheson sighed for poetic
prettiness and beribboned flattery that did not accompany her
rude caricatures and comic valentines. In "An Epistle to a
Lady, Who Desired the Author to Make Verses on Her, in the
Heroick Stile," 1733, Swift acts in character to have her plead
for loftier, gentler words:

> But, I beg, suspend a while,
> That same paultry burlesque stile:
> Drop, for once, your constant rule,
> Turning all to ridicule...
>
> . . .
> Sing my praise in strain sublime:
> Treat me not with doggrel rhime.
>   (49-52, 57-58)

But he has a refusal ready for her. His flattery has been spent
on Vanessa, his affection has been addressed to Stella, and
Daphne is to hear only raillery and must be pleased with that:

> Thus, I find it by experiment,

Scolding moves you less than merriment.
I may storm and rage in vain;
It but stupifies your brain.
But, with raillery to nettle,
Set your thoughts upon their mettle:
Gives your imagination scope,
Never lets your mind elope:
Drives out brangling, and contention,
Brings in reason and invention.
For your sake, as well as mine,
I the lofty stile decline.

                            (207-218)

4.

HARLEY AND SHERIDAN

Poems for other friends, though usually easy and smooth,
capable and adequate, do not have so much to recommend them
as those for Vanessa, Stella, and Daphne. They are all alike,
however, in drawing humor and delight from Swift's acting in
character, just as all his poems of wit are based on surprise
of situation or language. The poems addressed to Harley, Lord
Oxford, borrow some of the urbanity of Horace, whom they
imitate; and in them Swift draws an amusing portrait of himself. In "Part of the Seventh Epistle of the First Book of
Horace Imitated," 1713, Harley assumes the role of the patron
Philippus, and Vulteius is Swift. Ruined by the "Dues, pay-
ments, fees, demands and cheats" that accompany his patron's bounty, he pleads to be restored to his simple way of
living. He describes himself in this poem as he was first seen
at a bookstall by Harley, who insisted upon befriending him.
It is a portrait of himself as he thought, or hoped, he impressed others, with "some humour in his face," "an easy,
careless mien," and an inclination to do what he pleased.

"An Imitation of the Sixth Satire of the Second Book of
Horace," 1714, to which Pope made additions, is also concerned with Harley's patronage but has most to say about

Swift himself. Except for the noisy, name-calling passages
that Addison deleted from "Baucis and Philemon" this is the
first of the poems in which Swift, for humorous effect, has
people talking interruptedly in clamorous speeches, like bees
"humming in my ears." It begins with a nostalgic picture of
his desire for a handsome house in the country and comfort-
able means to maintain it—and then contrasts this with the
hectic "jostle" of the life at court. Among the most entertaining lines, reminiscent of noblemen's gossip recorded by
Proust, are those that set down the great Harley's trivial
conversation:

> 'Tis (let me see) three years and more,
> (October next, it will be four)
> Since Harley bid me first attend,
> And chose me for an humble friend:
> Would take me in his coach to chat,
> And question me of this and that;
> As, "What's a-clock?" And, "How's the wind?
> "Whose chariot's that we left behind?
> Or gravely try to read the lines
> Writ underneath the country signs;
> Or, "Have you nothing new today
> "From Pope, from Parnel, or from Gay?
> (63-74)

Although this parenthetical, colloquial, ironic passage can
be immediately identified as the work of Swift, it follows
closely after Horace's description of Maecenas.

Horace is again the model for the poem "To the Earl of
Oxford, Late Lord Treasurer. Sent to Him When He Was in the
Tower, Before His Tryal," 1716. This is a conscientiously
faithful rendering of a portion of Ode 2, Book III, beginning
with the line Wilfred Owen denounced as a lie: "Dulce et
decorum est pro patria mori." For Swift, hoping to give cour-
age to Harley after his impeachment, the line becomes:

> How blest is he, who for his country dies...

Under a separate heading of foolery, volatility, raillery, and
fun are the verses addressed to Thomas Sheridan, Swift's

Irish crony and the grandfather of Richard Brinsley Sheridan.
For something like twenty-five years the two men exchanged
flurries of rhymed letters, riddles, libels, pasquinades, and
trifles that must have been entertaining to send and receive,
though they often seem like naughty boys' tablet drawings in
Williams's edition of the poems, where they incongruously
appear in handsome format with numbered lines and scholarly
head- and footnotes. Silly as they generally are under solemn
consideration, they nevertheless include the charming "Mary
the Cook-Maid's Letter to Dr. Sheridan" and two or three
other items worth reading once. They are intentionally and
boastfully off-hand pieces: to one of them, thirty-eight lines
long, Swift appended the casual note: "Written, sign'd, and
seal'd, five minutes and eleven seconds after the receipt of
yours, allowing seven seconds for sealing and superscribing,
from my bed-side, just 11 minutes after 11, Sept. 15th 1718."
And to another he added: "I beg your pardon for using my left
hand, but I was in great haste, and the other hand was employed at the same time in writing some letters of business."
Experiment with rhyme and verse-form, usually tried first by
Sheridan and improved upon by Swift, is constant and, seen
all together, wearisome. But one of Swift's inventions is worth
setting down. Ancestry for the strained, prosy verses of Ogden
Nash and for W.S. Gilbert's "Lost Mr. Blake" can be seen in
the long, laughing, suspended lines of the letter "From Dr.
Swift to Dr. Sheridan, Dec. 14, 1719, 9 at Night":

> It is impossible to know by your letter whether the wine
>   is to be bottled to-morrow, or no.
> If it be, or be not, why did not you in plain English tell
>   us so?
> For my part, it was by meer chance I came back to sit
>   with the ladies this night.
> And, if they had not told me there was a letter from you,
>   and your man Alexander had not gone, and come back
>   from the Deanery, and the boy here had not been sent
>   to let Alexander know I was here, I should have missed
>   the letter outright.
>
>   (1-4)

As the letter continues, rolling out lines like carpets, such
devil-may-care rhymes as "vengeance" / "ten jaunts" further resemble the deliberate distortions of Gilbert and Nash
with their "lot of news" / "hypotenuse," "pelican" / "un-
Amelican," and "overemphasis" / "Memphasis."

5.

"VERSES ON THE DEATH OF DR. SWIFT"

For humor and mirth in what he wrote, Swift's best subject
is himself. Meticulously self-effacing in his prose, he goes
out of his way in poem after poem to name himself as "Dr.
S—t," "the Drapier," "Cadenus," or "the Dean." He writes
of his indignation, illness, disgust, and despair in resigned
amusement, less from any wish to be funny than simply because it is "too late to turn serious now."

Self-consciously, in "The Author upon Himself," 1714,
he tries to catch a reflection or to invent a portrait of the
character with which he wishes to be identified:

> S(wift) had the sin of wit, no venial crime;
> Nay, 'twas affirm'd, he sometimes dealt in rhime:
> Humour, and mirth, had place in all he writ:
> He reconcil'd divinity and wit.
> He mov'd, and bow'd, and talk't with too much grace;
> Nor shew'd the parson in his gait or face;
> Despis'd luxurious wines, and costly meat;
> Yet, still was at the tables of the great.
> Frequented lords; saw those that saw the Queen;
> At Child's or Truby's never once had been;
> Where town and country vicars flock in tribes,
> Secur'd by numbers from the lay-men's gibes;
> And deal in vices of the graver sort,
> Tobacco, censure, coffee, pride, and port.
>   (9-22)

The last couplet is humorously ironic in its clever dove-tailing of coffeehouse "vices" as abstract as the show of pride and tangible enough to be drunk or stuffed into a pipe. A later couplet in the poem provides a nice impression of court politics and intrigue, in which Swift was a figure sufficiently influential to be caressed by candidates and lords. It is a blending of the fastidious and gross, the courtly and vulgar; and the pause after the first syllable in each line gives the effect of a burlesqued minuet or a courtier's affected hesitation:

> Now, Delawere again familiar grows;
> And, in Swift's ear thrusts half his powder'd nose.
>
> (67-68)

This independent, graceful, worldly, humorous Swift, whether wholly real or in part imaginary, is sometimes transformed into another Swift of dark, animal force and invective humor. The following lines from "Holyhead," 1727, are among those he wrote in a note-book while awaiting passage to Dublin, where Stella lay ill. Suavity and refinement give way to impatience with the irony of the situation:

> Lo here I sit at holy head
> With muddy ale and mouldy bread
> All Christian vittals stink of fish
> I'm where my enemyes would wish
>
> . . .
>
> I never was in hast before
> To reach that slavish hateful shore
> Before, I always found the wind
> To me was most malicious kind
> But now the danger of a friend
> On whom my fears and hopes depend
> Absent from whom all Clymes are curst
> With whom I'm happy in the worst
> With rage impatient makes me wait
> A passage to the land I hate.
>
> (1-4, 19-29)

"Lo," in the first line, seems more an ironic pun on the word "low," to describe Swift's state of mind, than it does an in-

terjection. Asking to be beheld at his worst, he makes "ale,"
"bread," and "fish" turn dismal by contaminating them with
"mud," "mould," and "stink." The second line is almost too
pleasant to the ear to suit its intention, but the third is mar-
velously ugly with its spit-out *i*'s: "All Christian vittals
stink of fish." The scorn that falls on the word "fish" gives
it the heaviest emphasis in the first couplets. Any attempt
to "normalize" these remarkáble lines would be as ill-ad-
vised as the inevitable presumption, two hundred years from
now, of patient editors who will "normalize" the poems of
E.E. Cummings and Dylan Thomas. To alter is sometimes to
spoil; and to replace "holy head" with the proper "Holyhead" would shift the rhyme-stress to "mouldy" in the second
line, and would be absurd. The spelling here is a part of
style.

Style does not especially distinguish other autobiographical
poems like "In Sickness," 1714, "The Dean to Himself on St.
Cecilia's Day," 1730, "The Dean and Duke," 1734, or even
the deft little verses on "The Author's Manner of Living."
But it becomes an important consideration in the famous
"Verses on the Death of Dr. Swift." More than for almost any
other important poem in English, there has been difficulty
here in separating style from subject-matter and poem from
poet. The poem has exploitation of language, genuine rhetorical power, reasonable irony, dry humor, and particularized
observations on the way human beings act. There is an astonishing, teasing marriage of destructive satire and creative
poetry. Even if the verses could be read without biographical
concern, or with minimal concern for the poet's personality,
they would still impress the reader. If, however, Swift's
famous couplet

> Poor Pope will grieve a month; and Gay
> A week; and Arbuthnott a day

had been written by some little-known eighteenth-century
churchman named Dr. Shift, how famous would it now be? The
lines would sag limply in "Verses on the Death of Dr. Shift"
if they read like this:

> Poor Polk will grieve a month; and Jay

A week; and Higglesby a day.

Knowledge of Pope, Gay, and Arbuthnot, whom Swift names
in his couplet, lends something to the lines, but not everything, as the ugly-sounding substitutions make clear. Swift's
repeated p's in "Poor Pope," his alliteration in "grieve" and
"Gay," and, in the second line, variations on the sound of *a*
are matters of conscious versification.

"On the Death of Dr. Swift" seems in tone midway between
the polish of "The Author on Himself" and the indignation of
"Holyhead," midway, that is, between "He mov'd, and bow'd,
and talk't with too much grace" and "I'm where my enemyes
would wish." Force of passion, acute sensitiveness, bitterness, and laughter mingle to achieve the peculiar Swiftian
irony that drew envy even from Voltaire. The sane, preserva-
tive force of that irony shows itself best when one looks at
another poet's anticipation of death: Thomas Flatman, who
wrote on many of Swift's themes, imagined his own death without irony, humor, or even any dignity. Like Swift after him,
Flatman imagined his friends' conversation on his last day;
and thinking about it made him set up a terrified and dis-
tressing wail:

> Oh, the sad day,
> When friends shall shake their heads and say
> Of miserable me,
> Hark how he groans, look how he pants for breath,
> See how he struggles with the pangs of Death!

Swift neither screams nor groans. Much of the power of his
poem comes from its level tone, everyday language, and prosaic detail in a wholly imaginary situation. When a writer has
once created imaginary circumstances, there need be no limits
to his imagination; but for Swift the horrible nightmare of *A
Modest Proposal* is expressed with efficient, business-like
concern; his Gulliver moves through fantastic settings with
a perfectly convincing air of common sense; in "Baucis and
Philemon" the miracles are matter-of-fact and described precisely; and the deities' heavenly legal proceedings in "Cadenus and Vanessa" might have been taken from London court

records. In "Verses on the Death of Dr. Swift" irony shows
itself in the consummately maintained atmosphere of reality.

On the first of December, 1731, Swift wrote to Gay that he
had been "several months writing near five hundred lines on
a pleasant subject, only to tell what my friends and enemies
will say on me after I am dead. I shall finish it soon, for I
add two lines every week, and blot out four and alter eight."
The pleasant subject appeared in print first in oddly garbled
form as "The Life and Genuine Character of Doctor Swift,"
1733; then as "Verses on the Death of Doctor Swift Written
by Himself," 1739, with many alterations and deletions by
Pope and Dr. King; and finally in the genuine version under
Swift's direction as "Verses on the Death of Dr. Swift, D.S.P.
D. Occasioned by Reading a Maxim by Rochefoulcault. Dans
l'adversité de nos meilleurs amis nous trouvons quelque
chose, qui ne nous deplaist pas," 1739.

To begin, the poem announces its text in La Rochefoucauld's cynical philosophy of self-love and submits arguments
for proof:

> As Rochefoucault his maxims drew
> From nature, I believe 'em true:
> They argue no corrupted mind
> In him; the fault is in mankind.
>
> This maxim more than all the rest
> Is thought too base for human breast;
> "In all distresses of our friends
> "We first consult our private ends,
> "While nature kindly bent to ease us,
> "Points out some circumstance to please us.
>   (1-10)

This defense of La Rochefoucauld was Swift's way of de-
fending his own point of view. Both the Duke and Dean believed that Man had degenerated from a higher state toward
which he should climb upwards and spend his life in climb-
ing, though like Hobbes, Montaigne, and Boileau they knew
that the excellences of that higher state could never be re-
gained. Without illusions, they beheld a disenchanted world

and refused to apply beautiful, false names to its severe
realities. This same world, however, was not without a certain humor which allowed a duke or a dean to remark cleverly
upon its bitterest truths. In his "Thoughts on Various Subjects" Swift could occasionally be as cynical as La Rochefoucauld, though his observations are hardly so exquisitely
finished. "It is allow'd, that the cause of most actions, good
or bad, may be resolved into the love of our selves...," he
wrote in the manner of the *Maximes*. When he learned that
Pope intended to refute the principles of La Rochefoucauld,
he protested that those principles were his own:

> I tell you after all, that I do not hate mankind: it is
> *vous autres* who hate them, because you would have
> them reasonable animals, and are angry for being
> disappointed. I have always rejected that definition,
> and made another of my own. I am no more angry with
> (Walpole) than I was with the kite that last week
> flew away with one of my chickens; and yet I was
> pleased when one of my servants shot him two days
> after. This I say, because you are so hardy as to
> tell me of your intentions to write maxims in opposi-
> tion to Rochefoucauld, who is my favourite, because
> I found my whole character in him. However I will
> read him again, because I may have since undergone
> some alterations.

If he did reread the *Maximes*, he did not change his opinion;
for outside the allegory of *Gulliver's Travels* the most elo-
quent statement of his real feelings about mankind appears,
much as La Rochefoucauld might have put it in verse, in the
prophetic description of the effect of his funeral upon the
world.

Swift says that, like everyone else, he envies his acquaint-
ances (1-70); the story follows in brilliant scenes imagining
friends who remark on his decay and then "hug themselves"
because things are "not yet so bad" with them (71-146); then
the day of his death and shortly after (147-242); conversation
at the bookseller's when a year has passed (243-298); and a

long coffeehouse exposition of Swift's character by "One
quite indiff'rent in the cause" (299-484). Though he is ostensibly talking about himself, Swift has a good deal to say
about friendship, envy, and human relationships in general:
he observes how we hate to be outdone, how we tacitly con-
gratulate ourselves on escaping the misfortunes of our friends,
and how we would wish the odds always on our side. There
is deadly accuracy in these dry, humorous verses.

William Hazlitt did not err when he spoke of Swift's "ex-
quisite tone of irony" and his "touching, unpretending pathos,
mixed up with the most whimsical and eccentric strokes of
pleasantry and satire." It is mostly for these verses alone
that a crumb of admiration is sometimes thrown to Swift as
a poet. Biographers and critics, although they almost never
pause to analyze the poem, usually offer a polite serving
from it and remark on its "splendid lines," "remarkable
passages," and "glow and force of feeling." In Swift's own
time the poem on his death had great circulation and acclaim.
"In short," Dr. King wrote less than two months after its
publication, "all people read it, all agree to commend it, and
I have been well assured, the greatest enemies the Dean has
in this country(England), allow it to be a just and beautiful
satire."

> "Before the passing-bell begun,
> "The news thro' half the town has run.
> "O, may we all for death prepare!
> "What has he left? and who's his heir?
> "I know no more than what the news is,
> "'Tis all bequeath'd to publick uses.
> "To publick use! a perfect whim!
> "What had the publick done for him!
>   . . .
> Here shift the scene, to represent
> How those I love, my death lament.
> Poor Pope will grieve a month; and Gay
> A week; and Arbuthnott a day.
>
> St. John himself will scarce forbear,
> To bite his pen, and drop a tear.

> The rest will give a shrug and cry,
> I'm sorry; but we all must dye.
> Indifference, clad in Wisdom's guise,
> All fortitude of mind supplies:
> For how can stony bowels melt
> In those who never pity felt;
> When *we* are lash'd, *they* kiss the rod;
> Resigning to the will of God.
>
> The fools, my juniors by a year,
> Are tortur'd with suspense and fear.
> Who wisely thought my age a screen,
> When death approach'd, to stand between:
> The screen remov'd, their hearts are trembling,
> They mourn for me without dissembling.
>   (151-158, 205-224)

Though there is nothing oblique in these typical lines, they are by no means flat: personification appears in "Indifference" and "Wisdom"; there are figures of speech like "stony bowels," "kiss the rod," and "my age a screen"; and the rhetorical question (215-216) is effective. On examination, however, none of these devices seem very original or overwhelmingly witty. Like the time-tried phrase "fortitude of mind," which Swift uses here, they help to give the illusion of easy, familiar mood to the cynical observations he makes. In their mocking, humorous context they suit exactly. More inventive, however, are the wonderful lines that follow, probably the most deservedly famous in the poem:

> My female friends, whose tender hearts
> Have better learn'd to act their parts,
> Receive the news in doleful dumps,
> "The Dean is dead, (and what is trumps?)
> "The Lord have mercy on his soul.
> "(Ladies, I'll venture for the vole.)
> "Six deans, they say, must bear the pall.
> "(I wish I knew what king to call.)
> "Madam, your husband will attend
> "The funeral of so good a friend.
> "No madam, 'tis a shocking sight,

"And he's engag'd to-morrow night!
"My Lady Club wou'd take it ill,
"If he shou'd fail her at quadrill.
"He lov'd the Dean. (I lead a heart.)
"But dearest friends, they say, must part.
"His time was come, he ran his race;
"We hope he's in a better place.
                              (225-242)

In some of Hardy's "Satires of Circumstance," though seldom so ingenious, close-knit, and well sustained, there is a
kindred disclosure of callousness through light, animated conversation. Here the counterpoint of the ladies' card game, the
real business at hand, runs on serenely through their chatter
about their old friend's death; and rather than cluttering or
confusing the episode, their parenthetical remarks bring
variety in tone and pace. The contrasts and juxtapositions
carry irony on several planes. "The Dean is dead, (and what
is trumps?)," for example, combines disparate levels of concern and has an exact balance of phrases to oppose "Dean"
with "what" and "dead" with "trumps." This announcement
of death is ironically accompanied by a term from card play-
ing that is also, in the phrase "the last trump," the poetic
word for "trumpet." An identical pattern is followed in "He
lov'd the Dean. (I lead a heart.)," where there is opposition
of "lov'd" and "lead," "Dean" and "heart." There is poetic
irony again in the suggestion of analogy between pretended
love and a heart that is only a suit in a game of cards. In both
these lines, and through half the episode, there is closeness
of texture from echoed sounds.

Most important, by acting in character to speak for his
"female friends" on the imagined occasion of his death,
Swift hits off a scene to show the casual cruelty and farce of
life through humor that is not often surpassed. He wrote of
himself in the poem as "chearful to his dying day," but his
humor was neither that of a gaffer's snigger from a rocking-
chair nor a vestry-room giggle behind the starched sleeve of
a white lawn surplice: even when he laughed loudest or was

most ironic, he said he usually had a certain view in mind:

> "Perhaps I may allow, the Dean
> "Had too much satyr in his vein;
> "And seem'd determin'd not to starve it,
> "Because no age could more deserve it.
> "Yet, malice never was his aim;
> "He lash'd the vice but spar'd the name.
> "No individual could resent,
> "Where thousands equally were meant.
> "His satyr points at no defect,
> "But what all mortals may correct;
> "For he abhorr'd that senseless tribe,
> "Who call it humour when they jibe:
> "He spar'd a hump or crooked nose,
> "Whose owners set not up for beaux.
> "True genuine dulness mov'd his pity,
> "Unless it offer'd to be witty.
>
> (455-470)

CHAPTER THREE
SWIFT HAD THE SIN OF WIT

1.

SWIFT'S IDEA OF WIT

It was to punish him for his wit that caricatures of Jonathan Swift in his own day showed, beneath his churchly gown, a cloven devil's foot. Punishment of the same kind, he thought, withheld preferments from him, brought him the name of dangerous free-thinker, and banished him to his unwanted deanery in Dublin. Though he had hoped for a bishopric and was promised medals by the Queen, without them he still had wit brighter than a drawerful of medals. Speaking in the exasperated voice of experience that has fed on obstacles, the voice of wit that has suffered for the crime of being witty, Swift fixes the reader's eye to address him point-blank:

> Since there are persons who complain
> There's too much satire in my vein...
> ("A Dialogue between an Eminent
> Lawyer and Dr. Swift," 1-2)

. . .

Rightly you shew, that *wit* alone
Advances few, enriches none...
("A Panegyric on the Reverend
Dean Swift," 72-73)

. . .

So academick dull ale-drinkers
Pronounce all men of wit, free-thinkers.
("To Dr. Delany on the Libels,"
97-98)

. . .

"Had he but spared his tongue and pen,
"He might have rose like other men...
("Verses on the Death of Dr.
Swift," 356-357)

These lines, among others in the poetry, form a kind of essay on the price to be paid for wit. In his correspondence, too, the subject is a recurring one. When, out of his years and sickness and rage, he looked back at his career, he knew that he had written too much satirical poetry for his own good and that it had angered great people who might have done him favors. Nevertheless, when he sent advice to an overserious beginner in poetry, Swift pressed him to try for a vein of satire and a state of mind racier than he could find in Milton, who had been his model. Swift was, it is clear, recommending as a model his own poetry of inventive, surprising, and lashing wit:

As I am conjectured to have generally dealt in raillery and satire, both in prose and verse, if that conjecture be right, although such an opinion has been an absolute bar to my rising in the world, yet that very world must suppose that I followed what I thought to be my talent, and charitable people will suppose I had a design to laugh the follies of mankind out of countenance, and as often to lash the vices out of practice. And then it will be natural to conclude, that I have some partiality for such kind of writing, and favour it in others.

Though he had lost a mitre through dangerous wit, he still

urged its use to express contempt for whatever is ludicrous
and absurd. This was, he knew, a daring thing to recommend;
for men of wit are always looked upon with some suspicion.
The early eighteenth century was markedly a time of suspicion,
argument, and sense, in which the sensible men were method-
ical and utilitarian; believed in a reasonable age of progress;
and frowned steadily upon the men of wit. To cultivate scorn
and wantonly oppose progress with the counter-force of satire
seemed reprehensible. Witty play on words or ideas, or play
of almost any kind seemed, as it had to Bunyan, a thing to
check. Steele, who desired to be spokesman for the age, en-
couraged the scorning of scorn, saying that hearts are more
valuable than wits. In the Epilogue to *The Lying Lover* he
called laughter "a distorted passion" and recommended the
"gen'rous pity of a painted woe" as an emotion far more
heartfelt and sensible. The "bloody battle" between Wit and
Sense was chronicled in a long poem by Defoe early in his
career. He described the sallies by Blackmore and Collier
against the Wits, recounted Dennis's raids in reprisal, and
came to the conclusion that neither side could live alone:

> The Men of Sense against the Men of Wit,
> Eternal fighting must determine it.
>   . . .
> Wit is a king without a parliament,
> And Sense a democratic government:
> Wit, like the French, wher'e'er it reigns destroys,
> And Sense advanc'd is apt to tyrranize:
> Wit without Sense is like the laughing-evil
> And Sense unmix'd with fancy is the d—l.
>   (Defoe, "The Pacificator," 57-58, 365-370)

In Swift's own work, sense and wit were united. But the
men of sense still frowned. "...I have heard often affirmed
by innocent people, that too much wit is dangerous to salvation," Pope once wrote in a joking mood to Swift. Years later
and not jokingly, Thomas Gray wrote of himself: "No very
great wit, he believed in a God..." Many years later still,
using a different aspect of the word, Matthew Arnold did not
even smile when he condemned poetry of the wits because, he

said, "...genuine poetry is conceived in the soul."

If wit is dangerous, a barrier to success, a sin, a mark of godlessness, and lodged only in poetry that is a fraud, it would seem a thing to be avoided by poets who have any care for general acclaim. But in Swift's day, at least, it was pursued like gold and was less often captured, so that he cynically observed:

> All human race wou'd fain be wits,
> And millions miss, for one that hits.
> ("On Poetry: A Rapsody," 1-2)

Those who did not miss were the men we call the great ones of Swift's time, even though—as Pope's "innocent people" hoped was true—they may have forfeited heavenly salvation.

Wittily as their art allowed, pretenders to the title of poetic wit have sought to fix its changeable, shifty, inconstant meaning. For the most part they have had to concede that although wit is fine equipment for a poet, its definition does not come easily. Critics of literature, following the poets, have more confidently said what it might be. And categories, analyses, and explanations are set down by scholars following a distance after the critics.

In Shakespeare's time the usual meaning of wit was a spacious, generalized one of "wisdom," "sense," or "mind." But toward the middle of the seventeenth century when John Donne's songs and sonnets were published, it was a name for the poetic process itself and was particularly akin to what was known and courted as "fancy." Donne's was a wit of audacious surprise that saw poetic resemblances and analogies between the rarity of a comet and a woman's innocence, between pearls and the sweat-drops on his mistress' brow, and between a shattered mirror and his own heart. It was often brilliant conceit that could dazzle or blind or, often too, merely distract. In his *Leviathan*, 1651, Thomas Hobbes made a famous distinction between this "fancy" of resemblances and the "judgment" that shows differences in objects seemingly alike: ornaments and flowers, Hobbes said, grow from "fancy"; but the structure of the tree of verse itself is a thing of "judgment." For great poetry he would have them joined.

By the time of Abraham Cowley, whom Swift in his youth tried to imitate, wit could be thought of as structural, steady, and sober, nourished by the conscious faculties. Cowley's ode "Of Wit," 1656, describes a thing bearing a thousand different shapes but having orderliness of ideas and lending harmony and proportion to poetry. This dignifying point of view would have pleased Sir William Temple. By 1690, during Swift's decade of intermittent employment in his home, Sir William was out of patience with the pestilence of conceit, writing that it was like spangles hiding a gown, as frequent as rhyme in the "scribbles" of the day. Five years later, clever William Congreve, Swift's former schoolmate in Ireland, paused in his observations on humor in comedy to remark, less cleverly than usual, that though wit seemed to be the opposite of folly, like humor it could not be certainly defined. These were the years in which young Jonathan Swift, in his middle twenties, was publishing his first poem, in imitation of Cowley; addressing verses to Temple and Congreve; and writing about "the ambition of my wit," "the lost language, wit," and saying "We join like flyes, and wasps, in buzzing about wit," self-consciously hunting out "writ," "pit," "it," and "sit" for his rhyme.

Among the poets it remained for John Dryden, who is supposed to have scared the hankering for sublimity out of Cousin Swift, to write as an authority on the subject. Wishing to exchange surface-glitter and dancing conceits, however attractive they may be, for a manly, "boisterous English wit," Dryden praised that lively faculty of imagination "which like a nimble spaniel, beats over and ranges through the field of memory..." Yet when it came time for Swift's friend Joseph Addison to try his hand, Dryden's easy dictum was no longer acceptable. Observing like all the others how wit is admired but little understood, Addison found most satisfactory of all, the philosophical account by John Locke in which wit was shown to be a resemblance and congruity of ideas. Addison thought it necessary to remark, as he was at last separating

true wit from the false and mixed, that resemblances of ideas
are, after all, not wit unless for the reader they bring delight
and, especially, surprise: "Thus when a poet tells us the
bosom of his mistress is as white as snow, there is no wit in
the comparison; but when he adds, with a sigh, that it is as
cold too, it then grows into wit."

A dearer friend of Swift's among the poets might have
called his "Essay on Criticism" an "Essay on Wit" instead; for to Pope criticism, wit, and poetry were locked
inextricably. Like Cowley he would have poetic wit of harmony, order, and proportion; like Temple he expressed impatience with the ornament and trimming of pasted-on conceits; like Dryden he praised the powerful effect of "the
joint force and fell result of all"; and like Addison he appre-
ciated the art of manipulated surprise:

> True wit is nature to advantage dress'd,
> What oft was thought, but ne'er so well express'd;
> Something, whose truth convinc'd at sight we find,
> That gives us back the image of our mind.
> (Pope, "Essay on Criticism," 297-300)

Pope's description did not satisfy Dr. Johnson. A nobler
sort of wit, he felt, would express ideas, not of "What oft
was thought," but of "that which he that never found it won-
ders how he missed..." Dr. Johnson saw neither sort in the
work of Donne, Jonson, Cleveland, Cowley, and the other
poets he termed "metaphysical." To him, their wit seemed
merely an extravagance of language best exemplified by the
outlandish, wonderful puns extending through the most serious
poems of John Donne. Long before this wit of language had
received Johnson's depreciatory name of "metaphysical," it
had become somewhat out-moded. Even before the close of
the seventeenth century, especially in comedies for the stage,
it was a source for amusement. In the first scene of Shad-
well's *Bury-Fair*, 1689, Mr. Wildish remarks of Mr. Oldwit
that he is "a paltry old-fashioned wit, and punner of the last
age; that pretends to have been one of Ben Johnson's sons,
and to have seen plays at the Blackfryers."

The poetry of Swift is not so irreconcilably different from

the poetry of Donne and the sons of Ben as many literary historians have believed: both are poetry of wit. But wit for Swift was less a matter of style than a point of view. Donne's elegy called "Going to Bed" and Swift's "A Beautiful Young Nymph Going to Bed" are both poems that have been called indelicate and disgusting; they both describe the disrobing of a woman; and both are successful poems of wit. There could hardly be, however, two poems more patently unlike in their intention and effect. The audaciously physical metaphors, similes, and puns in the love-poem "Going to Bed" are centered in Donne's exultant cry of "Full nakedness!" Nakedness in "A Young Nymph Going to Bed" is made intentionally unattractive by enumeration of "artificial hair," "flabby dugs," and "running sores." There is a real similarity between Donne and Swift in certain passages from poems on their own deaths. This is a subject with which both poets were preoccupied: the first line of Donne's fourth "Satyre"— "Well! I may now receive, and die..." — could also serve for "Verses on the Death of Dr. Swift." But even when they are most alike, the two poets do not share quite the same kind of wit. In many of Swift's poems wit is more than a matter of style. Its purpose is often one of scorn; and Swift's scorn, in his poetry and prose as well, can be magnificent. For Donne wit was generally an artistic tool. For Swift it was more often employed as a weapon.

Swift himself accepted the title of "wit." In his earliest correspondence he wrote of "the wits" as coxcombs and macaronies; but by the time he had become a redoubtable figure in London, in the days of his political power, he had assumed the name for himself and was already jealous of others who wished to share it. "I hate to have any new witts rise," he wrote in the *Journal to Stella*; "but when they do rise I would encourage them, but they tread on our heels, & thrust us off the stage." When he was a veteran on that stage, he was still out of patience with aspirants to the name of wit, especially if their talent seemed to lie only in presumption. A dandyish young man once made the mistake of saying to him, with a gesture:

"You must know, Mr. Dean, that I set up for a wit."

"Do you so," said Swift; "then take my advice, and
sit down again."

Though he defined "wit," like Pope and the others he did
not always remember his definition, writing at one time of
wit and sense as a compatible pair, and elsewhere allying it
with elegance, judgment, joke, or virtue. Whatever company
it might keep, he praised it, saying in The Author's Apology
for *A Tale of a Tub*, that "wit is the noblest and most useful
gift of human nature..." When he qualified this, in a famous
sentence from *The Battle of the Books*, it was to disown as
true wit all that was giddy and smart without judgment to give
it body: "Wit, without knowledge, being a sort of cream, which
gathers in a night to the top, and, by a skilful hand, may be
soon whipped into froth; but, once scummed away, what appears underneath will be fit for nothing but to be thrown to
the hogs."

He went further to differentiate from humor and raillery the
inventive wit of the intellect that could not be merely scummed
away, though he was particular to say that he was erecting no
boundaries of definition:

> (Wit), as boundless as the wind;
> Is well conceiv'd thô not defin'd;
> For, sure, by wit is onely meant
> Applying what we first invent...
> For wit and humor differ quite,
> That gives surprise, and this delight...
>   ("To Mr. Delany," 15-18, 23-24)

Swift was thinking here of the invention and surprise in conversational wit, but his poetry is itself so remarkably conversational, often in the form of monologue and dialogue, that
what he says is appropriate to "Baucis and Philemon," "The
Day of Judgement," and all his other sly, satirical, and unexpected wit-in-rhyme. By prescribing invention and surprise
for true wit, he was not drawing upon the Cowleyan idea of
harmony and proportion of intellect and the senses so much
as upon a concept like Addison's. If he had invented the
simile of snow to describe a mistress' bosom, he would have

done so for the sake of mischievous parody; but he would
have gone on, like Addison, to make wit of the simile. Wit,
he told Dr. Delany, "is a quick-sighted faculty, which finds
out allusions and resemblances of things, seemingly most
distant and unlike: and when it hath found them out, its
greatest delight is to shew them: and therefore can seldom
resist the pride, and pleasure of doing so; be the subject
what it will, or the occasions never so improper."

Because Swift was the man he was, his subject for wit and
its occasion were seldom so uninventive and without surprise
as the description of a mistress' bosom in clever society
love-verse. When he wrote with most endearment of Stella, it
was to liken her, and rather movingly, to a weather-beaten
sign, a badger, or a cow. Most often his wit in poetry and
prose was in the form of satirical comment, perhaps startlingly point-blank or sometimes wickedly roundabout, on whatever offended his good sense. Even when he wrote in a burst
of spite on "occasions never so improper," or intentionally
to vex the world, he wrote with keen and imaginative wit that
grew out of invention of the mind and was colored, sometimes
almost alarmingly, with brilliant surprises.

2.

THE PATTERN FOR "THE DAY OF JUDGEMENT"

In all Jonathan Swift's poems, though it is especially ap-
parent in the briefer ones, wit often lies in juxtapositions no
less surprising than T.S. Eliot's use of "garlic," "sapphires,"
and "mud" in a single line. Many of these poems by Swift,
which are almost perfect of their kind and should be better
known, depend upon a final line or two for their chief effect
through sudden contrast of the literary and colloquial, etherial and earthy. Such a poem is "The Power of Time," 1727.
Its subject is as familiar in the world of poetry as the charm
of Beauty and the triumph of Death: even stone and brass,
poems on the subject remind us, do not last for ever. In
Shakespeare's sonnet it sounds like this: "Since brass, nor

stone, nor earth, nor boundless sea, / But sad mortality o'er-
sways their power...''; and Swift's friend Thomas Parnell
echoes with: "Relentless Time! destroying power. / Whom
stone and brass decay..." Now when the reader of Jonathan
Swift's poetry sees in measured lines, solemnly musical, the
old accepted phrases for a poem on the power of Time, he
should be wary. He must no more settle back to be lulled by
familiar apothegm than settle back to learn geography from
what disarmingly purports to be *Travels into Several Remote
Nations of the World, in Four Parts.*

The Power of Time

> If neither brass nor marble can withstand
> The mortal force of Time's destructive hand;
> If mountains sink to vales, if cities die
> And lessening rivers mourn their fountains dry;
> When my old cassock, says a Welch divine,
> Is out at elbows, why should I repine?

The query of the final lines, rushing after pretentious
stresses that have preceded, brings the unexpected in a hurry.
From the abstract, grand, and "poetic" of his parody Swift
has turned in an instant to the common and specific: Time's
mortal force, death of cities, and the end of rivers are themselves paradoxically destroyed by the image, brought close
before the reader's eyes, of a cassock threadbare from use.
And it is after the spread-out literary elegance of marble,
vales, and fountains, when we might expect to read at least
of "priestly robes," that we are surprised back into an inelegant world with the homely phrase "out at elbows."

Though this brief poem opens with mellifluous couplets that
mimic pretentious poetry almost too exactly, the query of the
Welshman comes as a relief as well as a surprise. It is the
expected unexpected. The effect is certainly no accident, for
we know that Swift revised the lines to achieve his end. As
he tentatively wrote them they were:

> When *the* old cassock *of* a Welch divine
> Is out at elbows why should *he* repine?

In that form the surprise is less, and the effect is not so immediate: it is second-hand, with the speaker still in the middle-distance rather than talking in the first-person-singular as he is in the finished poem—talking at the reader's side.

The twist from remote to immediate, impersonal to personal, lofty to colloquial, sententious to witty, unreal to real, is adeptly manipulated in the six lines of this light verse. But it is not necessarily inconsequential because it is light. In his sonnet "Since Brass nor Stone," Shakespeare says that as Time destroys all things, Beauty cannot survive except, perhaps, in the expression of love immortalized in his sonnet itself. What Swift is saying seems at least as wise and memorable: that since all things decay, even impersonal things we call indestructible, it is useless to complain of losses that are merely personal.

Variations on the device of witty turnabout are familiar in brief fiction like that of Maupassant and in ironic verses like Thomas Hardy's "Satires of Circumstance" where a concluding phrase may abruptly reveal a preacher's vanity, a bride's domination by an old love, or a lifetime of misunderstanding. For Swift the device takes several forms: there are brief poems which turn suddenly in their conclusion from lofty to colloquial style; certain epigrammatic verses intended to surprise; and a few important poems that seem successful parodies largely because of their concluding lines.

Of the first sort is the poem "On His Deafness," 1734, which follows the same pattern as "The Power of Time" to cause surprise. In Swift's correspondence his complaints of vertigo, deafness, and head-noises show that he was often in physical discomfort and that it was a matter that tormented him. Yet in eight lines he uses wit to describe his situation. "Deaf, giddy, helpless, left alone" might in other hands have introduced observations like those that follow Milton's "When I consider how my light is spent," or it might merely have aroused pity by a catalogue of infirmities. But this is poetry of wit that suddenly thrusts a fool's cap on the hero's head or snatches away the beau's fine wig to show him bald.

On His Deafness

Deaf, giddy, helpless, left alone,
To all my friends a burthen grown,
No more I hear my church's bell,
Than if it rang out for my knell:
At thunder now no more I start,
Than at the rumbling of a cart:
Nay, what's incredible, alack!
I hardly hear a woman's clack.

Without the final line even the rather well-turned remark on
his funeral bell does not make the poem a witty one. It is
the single colloquial word "clack," like the phrase "out at
elbows" in "The Power of Time," that brings full surprise
into the lines. If rhyme allowed substitution of the word "talk"
for "clack," the wit would vanish and interest would lie
chiefly in Swift's willingness to find amusement in verses on
his deafness, giddiness, and old age.

Though a third poem and one better known, "The Place of
the Damn'd," 1731, depends upon Swift's contrast of style
and mood, there is amusement of a different sort in its final
two lines; for they conclude a poem of such cumulative violence that even the relief of a sudden, quietly conversational
ending does not dispel it. The furious insistent drumming of
the *d*'s in "damn'd," repeated eighteen times in as many
lines, can still be heard when the poem is finished.

The Place of the Damn'd

All folks who pretend to religion and grace,
Allow there's a Hell, but dispute of the place;
But if Hell may by logical rules be defin'd,
The Place of the Damn'd,—I'll tell you my mind.
    Wherever the damn'd do chiefly abound,
Most certainly there is the Hell to be found,
Damn'd poets, damn'd critics, damn'd block-heads, damn'd
        knaves,
Damn'd senators brib'd, damn'd prostitute slaves;
Damn'd lawyers and judges, damn'd lords and damn'd
        squires,

Damn'd spies and informers, damn'd friends and damn'd
    lyars;
Damn'd villains, corrupted in every station,
Damn'd time-serving priests all over the nation;
And into the bargain, I'll readily give you,
Damn'd ignorant prelates, and councellors privy.
Then let us no longer by parsons be flamm'd,
For we know by these marks, the place of the damn'd;
And Hell to be sure is at Paris or Rome,
How happy for *us*, that it is not at home.

The sardonic impression left by the poem comes from invective suddenly changed to mock-fatuous mimicry of what might
be expressed by a self-righteous householder. "How happy
for *us*" can hardly be read aloud without an imitation of a
smirk. But the fierce accusal in "Damn'd ignorant prelates"
and "Damn'd time-serving priests," for instance, makes light
verse seem a misnomer: it disturbs and vexes, precisely as
Swift often said he intended, and as the modern "light verse"
of E.E. Cummings can disturb when he says what he thinks
about politicians, anthologists, and salesmen.

It too is devilishly witty, but there is nothing amusing
whatsoever in "The Day of Judgement," the most powerful
of Swift's briefer poems. In it the device of surprise by contrast is almost the same as that in "The Place of the Damn'd";
but when higher language drops to the colloquial here, the
poem's anger is intensified. Surely it is anger as unrelieved,
even by wit, as that in any other twenty-two rhymed lines in
English; and yet the poem is one of wit.

The choice of subject does not make it so: Thackeray un-
intentionally demonstrates this when he holds up "The Day
of Judgement" alongside prose extracts from Addison and
Steele, intending to place Sir Richard to advantage. He
imagines a mad, terrible Swift "stamping on a grave and carrying his scorn for mankind actually beyond it" and imagines
Swift saying: "Miserable, purblind wretches, how dare you
pretend to comprehend the Inscrutable...?" Beside him,
Thackeray tells us, is Addison, "smiling over the tombstones,
and catching, as is his wont, quite a divine effulgence as he

looks heavenward..." But Sir Richard Steele "leads you up
to his father's coffin, and shows you his beautiful mother
weeping, and himself an unconscious little boy wondering at
her side. His own natural tears flow, as he takes your hand
and confidingly asks your sympathy. 'See how good and innocent and beautiful women are,' he says, 'how tender little
children! Let us love these and one another, brother...'"
To avoid the embarrassment of Steele's own natural tears the
modern reader hastens back with new respect for the "terrible
lines of Swift," ready to help him stamp on graves.

When Thomas Flatman and Isaac Watts wrote on the same
theme in verse, they did not have wit in mind. "A Dooms-Day
Thought: Anno 1659" leads through Flatman's graveyard
imaginings and his attempts to intimidate ("who can dwell /
With everlasting burnings!") to his climactic admonition: on
Judgement Day it will be too late to mend our ways. In Watts's
"Day of Judgment: An Ode Attempted in English Sapphick,"
the verse-form holds more interest than what is being said.
Here too the reader is meant to be intimidated by "Hark the
shrill outcries of the guilty wretches!" and "Thoughts like
old vultures prey upon their heartstrings" until the poet bids
his fancy stop, cries "Come arise to Jesus," and concludes
with enthusiastic smugness in the language of prayer-meetings
and revivals.

"The Day of Judgement" bearing Swift's name is unlike
the work of Flatman, Watts, or anyone else than Swift. He
had, however, been dead for almost thirty years before it was
first printed—under circumstances that remain one of the most
intriguing pieces of unfinished business in literary history.
On August 27, 1752, Lord Chesterfield wrote to Voltaire that
he was sending him a poem on "Jupiter, au jour du jugement,"
copied from Swift's unpublished manuscript in Chesterfield's
possession. "Son Jupiter," he added to flatter Voltaire,
"...les traite à peu près comme vous les traitez, et comme
ils le meritent," And on November 21, 1756, Chesterfield
quoted from Swift's poem in a letter to the Bishop of Water-
ford: "The mad business of the world (as Swift says) is over
with me." But when the letter to Voltaire was first published
in Chesterfield's *Letters*, April 7, 1774, no poem accompanied

it. The poem appeared almost simultaneously, however, in the
St. James's Chronicle for April 9-12, 1774, with a prefatory
note referring to Chesterfield's *Letters*, and mysteriously
signed "Mercutio." Who "Mercutio" was, why he did not reveal himself, how he came into possession of the poem, and
whether he may not have written it himself in imitation of
Swift, are questions scholars who track down such matters
have been unable to answer. Swift is, nevertheless, almost
as certainly the author of "The Day of Judgement" as Shakespeare is of *King Lear*. The pattern for the poem is typical of
his ingenious verses that suddenly, through legerdemain of
style, assume a new identity on the page while the reader
watches.

The Day of Judgement

With a whirl of thought oppress'd,
I sink from reverie to rest.
An horrid vision seiz'd my head,
I saw the graves give up their dead.
Jove, arm'd with terrors, burst the skies,
And thunder roars, and light'ning flies!
Amaz'd, confus'd, its fate unknown,
The world stands trembling at his throne.
While each pale sinner hangs his head,
Jove, nodding, shook the heav'ns, and said,
"Offending race of human kind,
By nature, reason, learning, blind;
You who thro' frailty step'd aside,
And you who never fell—*thro' pride*;
You who in different sects have shamm'd,
And come to see each other damn'd;
(So some folks told you, but they knew
No more of Jove's designs than you)
The world's mad business now is o'er,
And I resent these pranks no more.
I to such blockheads set my wit!
I damn such fools!—Go, go, you're bit."

Though some critics have said that tormented hours of
skepticism, leading to madness, are reflected in these lines,

it is more useful to observe that the lines reflect a very conscious ability to create a startling poetic effect through versification and language. Swift does not ride an octosyllabic
rocking-horse but alters and shifts the verbal pattern to fit
his mood and meaning. If the first line, for instance, were in
regular iambic meter, with four evenly-spaced stresses, as in
"A WHIRL of THOUGHT my MIND opPRESS'D," there would
be no conviction whatever in the word "whirl." Swift's leading in with a hurried anapest makes the difference. In the
fifth and tenth lines, where Jove, "arm'd" and "nodding,"
enters the poem, there are heavy stresses made longer by
pauses within the lines. Aloud, at least, the tenth line requires almost twice as long to read as the first.

In employing wit to uncover irreligion that calls itself
piety, "The Day of Judgement" shows a furious Jove who
speaks in language befitting a god, even in the contemptuous
"pranks" to describe Man's childish hypocrisies, until the
fierce concluding couplet, where the language is that of
colloquial speech. Whereas Jove has spoken of himself in
the remote third-person ("Jove's designs"), he is now ter-
rifyingly near us, using our own speech, in first-person
phrases of "I resent," "I . . . set my wit," and "I damn." The
Jove who had shaken the heavens has come too close for
comfort; he has become, especially in the furious monosylla-
bic final line, Jonathan Swift himself, periwigged, and cry-
ing "Go, go, you're *bit.*"

When he was young and liked a new phrase to amuse, Swift
wrote to a friend: "I will teach you a way to outwit Mrs. Johnson: it is a new-fashioned way of being witty, and they call
it a *bite.* You must ask a bantering question, or tell some
damned lie in a serious manner, and then she will answer or
speak as if you were in earnest; and then cry you, 'Madam,
there's a *bite.*'" *You're bit,* spoken in cold disgust by a Jove
ready in dreadful sport to condemn or abandon all mankind,
is certainly not amusing, though it is still witty and still
part of Comedy. For Comedy, like that of another age in which
Thomas Hardy's Jove has himself become irresponsible and
the Godhead no longer has a brain, is not always amusing.

3.

EPIGRAMS

In certain shorter poems, concise, and pointed like arrows, the wit is epigrammatic. Observations on subjects like the English tongue, Irish sense, or violent wives, these epigrams hit their mark precisely. Swift's "Epigram on Scolding" bears no date of composition in Williams's edition of the poems, but certain phrases in it closely resemble those in a letter from William Pulteney, written to Swift on February 9, 1731. Pulteney was reporting on Dr. Arbuthnot's "Brief Account of Mr. John Ginglicut's Treatise concerning the Altercation or Scolding of the Ancients," and he told how Arbuthnot had amused himself by pretending to assign classical dignity to the mud-pie-war of invective in contemporary English pamphlets. "He shows," Pulteney wrote, "how the gods and goddesses used one another—dog, bitch, and whore, were pretty common expressions among them..." Swift's similar phrases are witty and mocking:

> Great folks are of a finer mold;
> Lord! how politely they can scold;
> While a coarse *English* tongue will itch,
> For whore and rogue; and dog and bitch.

Better known, with the same kind of exclamatory irony, is the quatrain on Irish sense. Familiar in biographies and studies of Swift, it is intended to show how, in the years when his mind had failed, his former intelligence gleamed brightly for a minute when he saw the armory in Phoenix Park and wrote in his pocket-book:

> Behold! a proof of Irish sense!
> Here Irish wit is seen!
> When nothing's left, that's worth defence,
> We build a magazine.

In the early pages of *Finnegans Wake*, through which the indignant ghost of Swift moves restlessly, James Joyce uses this epigram in disguised form. In the first line, printed as

prose, "Behold" is changed to "Behove"; and Swift's "proof"
becomes "sound" in H.C. Earwicker's wonderful dream.

As tersely as he wrote about the English tongue and Irish
sense, Swift put down rhymes on marriage or, more exactly,
on women who manhandle their men. There are three of these
epigrams, all transcribed in Stella's hand. The briefer ones,
beginning "When Margery chastises Ned" and "Joan cudgells
Ned, yet Ned's a bully," depend for their wit upon eighteenth-
century slang like "combs his head," "finds him horn," and
"cully." The third, though perhaps earliest in composition,
ends with the surprising, cynical wit that characterizes a good
epigram, here repeating a phrase from the first line to add
full circle to the surprise. It is a pattern that turns on itself:

> As Thomas was cudgell'd one day by his wife,
> He took to the street, and fled for his life:
> Tom's three dearest friends came by in the squabble,
> And sav'd him at once from the shrew and the rabble;
> Then ventur'd to give him some sober advice,
> But Tom is a person of honor so nice
> Too wise to take counsel, too proud to take warning,
> That he sent to all three a challenge next morning.
> Three duels he fought, thrice ventur'd his life;
> Went home, and was cudgell'd again by his wife.

Th.s is reminiscent of the undeluded, rough-tongued epigrams
of Thomas Hardy. But the author of "Verses on the Death of
Dr. Swift" and "The Day of Judgement" was writing here,
offhand, to entertain friends of an evening with wine or to
show how neatly he could crystallize a witty observation in
miniature.

4.

"DESCRIPTION OF A CITY SHOWER"
AND
"BAUCIS AND PHILEMON"

Still other poems by Swift are notable because of endings
which make clear, suddenly, that one has been reading parody

all along and that what has perhaps been taken seriously was really spoken through a mask. "The Power of Time," in which solemnly poetic lines turn into a Welsh preacher's observation on his poverty, is a good example. But that poem is not revealed as so obvious a parody as are two of Swift's longer, more masterly, and better-known poems, his "Description of a City Shower" and "Baucis and Philemon."

Early in October, 1710, he wrote to Stella about his "poetical 'Description of a Shower in London'" for the *Tatler*, later added that it was finished, "all but the beginning," and then reported that the missing lines had been supplied. Finally, on the seventeenth of October, he wrote: "This day came out the *Tatler*, made up wholly of my 'Shower,' and a preface to it. They say it is the best thing I ever writ, and I think so too." He pressed Stella for her opinion of the poem; and he was delighted when Rowe and Prior "both fell commending my 'Shower' beyond anything that has been written of the kind: there never was such a 'Shower' since Danaë's, etc..." His verses on the morning, Swift himself insisted, were "not half so good." There had been no such delight and wish for approval in his references to his essays and other works in prose, though many of them received approval, and deserved it. There had hardly been such a show of eagerness since his youthful letter to his cousin in which he confessed his ambition to sing odes like Cowley's. But now he was a more cynical Swift; youthful eagerness, which he patronized in others, had for himself evaporated.

Like many of his best poems "A Description of a City Shower" is in Swift's racy, almost anti-"poetic" style, with swarming realistic detail. Its last three lines give the show away, however, when the admirably realistic turns suddenly to open-faced parody: the author has been artfully fooling with the reader, as he does in *Gulliver's Travels* and *A Modest Proposal*. There are three levels to the poem. It is an evocation of what a rainstorm in eighteenth-century London was like; it is a criticism of all romantic and all dishonest description of nature; and its ending is specifically a parody of Dryden's favorite Alexandrines and triplet-rhymes. In the 1735 edition of the poems the "Shower" bears a note to just this effect; and in a letter, Swift wrote that "I was so angry at these corruptions that above twenty-four years ago I banished them all by one triplet, with the Alexandrine, upon a very ridiculous subject."

The poem is in four unframed vignettes that show the presentiment of rain, its preliminary sprinkle, the downpour, and the flood. As the shower grows, so does the wit. There is only a hint in the third line, with a suspicious use of the word "pensive," so familiar in serious Augustan elegies, that this is mock-heroic verse; for Swift's "pensive" describes a cat. Plumbing that stinks and corns that pain increase the suspicion that this is mockery of romantic nature-poetry, and the reader should be on to the joke by the time he begins the second division of the "Shower":

> Mean while the South rising with dabbled wings,
> A sable cloud a-thwart the welkin flings,
> That swill'd more liquor than it could contain,
> And like a drunkard gives it up again.
>   (13-16)

Probably the weakest in the poem, these plug-ugly lines are at the same time its strongest example of Swiftian juxtaposition meant to surprise. Deliberately hackneyed "poetical" phrases lead into phrases that are as deliberately un-"poetical" in subject and sound. "Swill'd" has the same relationship to "sable cloud" as the poem's concluding lines have to the poem itself.

Although that conclusion is the most famous part of the "Shower," and the part with which Swift thought he had "banished" certain corruptions from English poetry, the middle sections of the poem are what other writers might envy most. With easy thrift of words they sketch line-drawings of people in the rain or keeping out of it: a maid, a poet, shoppers, a barrister, a sempstress, Tories and Whigs, and an impatient dandy. In wittily describing people Swift is at his best. Humanizing everywhere—even in his prose on philosophy, politics, religion, and literature—he invented people (or sometimes animals) to act out and say for him what he wanted to say, and called them Jack, Peter, Martin, Isaac Bickerstaff,

Martin Scriblerus, M.B. Drapier, Lord Sparkish, or the Emperor
of Lilliput. He drew Lemuel Gulliver, for instance, so well
that readers have sometimes been diverted from what Gulliver
is intended to tell them. Here are his Londoners in the rain:

> Now in contiguous drops the flood comes down,
> Threat'ning with deluge this devoted town.
> To shops in crouds the daggled females fly,
> Pretend to cheapen goods, but nothing buy.
> The Templer spruce, while ev'ry spout's a-broach,
> Stays till 'tis fair, yet seems to call a coach.
> The tuck'd-up sempstress walks with hasty strides,
> While streams run down her oil'd umbrella's sides.
> Here various kinds by various fortunes led,
> Commence acquaintance underneath a shed.
> Triumphant Tories, and desponding Whigs,
> Forget their feuds, and join to save their wigs.
> Box'd in a chair the beau impatient sits,
> While spouts run clatt'ring o'er the roof by fits ...
>   (31-44)

Beginning with "contiguous," which falls into the poem as
heavily as the cloudburst it is meant to suggest, there is a
good deal in these lines that is skilfully arranged. Especially
tight-packed, like Hogarth's bright engraving "Noon," are the
heroic couplets with their group-portrait of bespattered shoppers and the full-length single portrait of the hurrying sempstress whose exact way of walking, arrangement of dress, and
(still more closely observed) wet umbrella require only a few
phrases. Though the compactness comes in part from expert
use of heroic couplets, there are other devices, and a determination to be succinct. Alliteration in almost every line and
even repetition of syllables and whole words gives an effect
of interweaving: "*various* kinds .... *various* fortunes" and
"While rain dePENds, the PENsive cat gives o'er," for instance. Swift's skill is doubly evident when one turns for
comparison to John Gay's *Trivia, or The Art of Walking the
Streets of London*, in which he tried, as pliantly as he tried
everything, to imitate Swift's "Shower." Though it is Gay's
best-remembered poem, and a lively handbook on eighteenth-

century manners, *Trivia* is partly buried under the peraphrasis
from which Swift was so wonderfully free. Swift's phrase
"swelling kennels" becomes Gay's "the kennels swell";
"oil'd umbrella's sides" becomes "th' umbrella's oily shed";
and "spouts run clatt'ring" becomes "spouts on heedless
men their torrents pour." When Gay comes to write of the
housewives' overshoes, he cannot get past them ("But, O!
forget not, Muse, the patten's praise"), and his episode on
their invention continues for seventy lines, tiresome even in
mock-heroic.

  If Swift had concluded with these pen-sketches of Londoners in the rain, he would not have written the poem that was
"beyond anything that has been written of the kind," or that
ridiculed out of existence the poetic "corruptions" Dryden
had fostered, or that caused Hippolyte Taine to protest "toutes
ces ordures." The eddying momentum of the last eleven lines
of Swift's poem increases to whirl his descriptive sketches
along with the drowned puppies and dung that offended Taine.
The whirlpool of the final triplet is meant to offend so that
Dryden's lines like these, conspicuously decorated with brack-
ets, will be forever distasteful:

>   'Twas fram'd, at first, our oracle t'enquire;
>   But, since our sects in prophecy grow higher,
>   The text inspires not them; but they the text inspire.

                          · · ·

>   What curses on thy blasted name will fall!
>   When age to age their legacy shall call;
>   For all must curse the woes that must descend on all.
>   (Dryden, "The Medal," 164-166, 260-262)

To ridicule this, Swift gives us an unlovely triple-rhyme of
"blood," "mud," and "flood," with a tumble of dead cats
and turnip-tops swirling in the long final Alexandrine of which
he disapproves:

>   Now from all parts the swelling kennels flow,
>   And bear their trophies with them as they go:
>   Filth of all hues and odours, seem to tell
>   What streets they sail'd from, by the sight and smell.

They, as each torrent drives, with rapid force
From Smithfield, or St. Pulchre's shape their course,
And in huge confluent join at Snow-Hill Ridge,
Fall from the conduit prone to Holborn-Bridge.
Sweepings from butchers' stalls, dung, guts, and blood, ⎫
Drown'd puppies, stinking sprats, all drench'd in mud, ⎬
Dead cats, and turnip-tops come tumbling down the flood. ⎭

Though the "Shower" was advertised as an imitation of
Virgil's Georgics, it is less obviously an imitation than
"Baucis and Philemon," 1709. Both are less accurately imitations than they are parodies. When Swift's tongue-in-cheek
tale of Baucis and Philemon is read alongside its versions
from less mischievous hands, the parody shows through. In
Shakespeare's time the most popular of ancient poets was
Ovid, most popularly translated by Arthur Golding, who is
nowadays of interest because Shakespeare picked here and
there among his verses to make better ones. When Golding
comes to the end of Ovid's "Baucis and Philemon," from the
eighth book of the Metamorphoses, he provides a suitable
moral to be carried away as a memento of what happened
"upon the hills of Phrygie." Golding's two honest, devoted
peasants have shared "simple poverty" of coleworts, bacon,
wild berries, endive, radishes, eggs, "a jolly lump of butter,"
nuts, dates, figs, apples, prunes, plums, grapes, honey, and
wine with strangers who turn out to be Jove and Mercury; and,
for reward, their straw hut becomes a temple, they are priest
and priestess, and they finally die together as they had con-
jugally wished, changing into trees, which had not been in
the bargain. In the Phrygian park, says Golding,

I saw the garlands hanging on the boughs, and adding new
I said, "Let them, whom God doth love, be gods, and honour due
Be given to such as honour him with fear and reverence
  true."

This is rather charming. Dryden, sharp-witted satirist though
he was, was charmed by "this good-natured story," as he
called it, and translated it like an exercise from Latin, con-

cluding:

> And off'ring fresher up with pious prayer,
> The good, said I, are God's peculiar care,
> And such as honour heaven, shall heavenly honour share.   }

Swift will have none of this. He is spoofing it throughout
his "Baucis and Philemon," where the scene is rural Kent,
the gods are merely saints, the fare is bacon and beer, Philemon is first transformed into a threadbare parson, Baucis
becomes "Madam" in black satin, and they are at last metamorphosed into yew-trees:

> Till once, a parson of our town
> To mend his barn, cut Baucis down;
> At which, 'tis hard to be believ'd,
> How much the other tree was griev'd:
> Grew scrubby, dy'd a-top, was stunted:
> So, the next parson stubb'd and burnt it.
>
> (173-178)

"Stubb'd and burnt it" bluntly and wittily replaces Ovid's
garlands in intertwined branches and, through Golding and
Dryden, "reverence true" and "God's peculiar care." Compared to "garlands hanging on the boughs," there is a kind of
insult and cruelty in "stubb'd and burnt it" —and a kind of
honesty and wit that we like to call modern.

Two episodes in the poem, besides the last, seem worth
examining. The metamorphosis of the cottage into a church
is as visually imaginative and surrealistic as some of T.S.
Eliot's metaphors; scenes from Gulliver's third voyage; or
Hogarth's frontispiece to Kirby's *Perspective*, in which a
woman leans from a window to hold a candle to the pipe of
a traveler on a distant hill, a bird is almost as large as its
tree, and the church seems to be crawling into the river:

> Aloft rose ev'ry beam and rafter;
> The heavy wall climb'd slowly after.
>   The chimney widen'd and grew higher,
> Became a steeple with a spire.
>
> . . .

> The groaning chair was seen to crawl,
> Like a huge snail half up the wall;
> There stuck aloft in publick view;
> And with small change, a pulpit grew.
>   (53-56, 85-88)

Further changes just as grotesque and deliberate turn the
kitchen kettle into a church bell, the roasting-jack into a
steeple clock, and the bedstead into pews where people still
may sleep. But in the second metamorphosis, when old Baucis
and Philemon branch and bud into yew-trees, disconcertedly
talking as they bud, Swift writes more characteristically, fit-
ting easy, exclamatory conversation to the requirements of
rhyme and meter as he later did so wonderfully in the verses
on his death and other poems:

> They went by chance, amidst their talk,
> To the church-yard, to fetch a walk:
> When Baucis hastily cry'd out,
> My dear, I see your forehead sprout!
> Sprout, quoth the man, what's this you tell us?
> I hope you don't believe me jealous:
> But yet, methinks, I feel it true;
> And really, yours is budding too—
> Nay,—now I cannot stir my foot;
> It feels as if 'twere taking root.
>   (153-162)

Though "Baucis and Philemon," even with its inescapably
rude ending of "stubb'd and burnt it," is one of the few
Swiftian poems critics have called lovable, they have taken
most interest in what it reveals of Addison's attempt to
smooth his friend into a more acceptable, properer poet. In
this attempt Addison was, luckily for Swift, in the long run
unsuccessful; but when he took this poem critically in hand,
before it was printed, he found fault with many of its lines,
so that Swift is recorded as saying that "Mr. Addison made
him blot out fourscore, add fourscore, and alter fourscore."
The portion of the manuscript in Swift's hand, now in the
Morgan Library, is longer by fifty-two lines, and is livelier

by almost as many, than the corresponding version that was
refined and dignified to please Addison. The lines thrown out
were largely Swiftian give-and-take of conversation between
wandering saints and unhospitable householders they call
"a pack of churlish boors." Probably the poem did not suffer
from deletion of

> One surly clown lookt out and said,
> I'll fling the p — pot on your head....

or

> They call'd at ev'ry dore; Good people,
> My comrade's blind, and I'm a creeple.

But it was overnice counsel that changed a phrase like "went
clamb'ring" to "climb'd slowly after" in the description of
the metamorphosed wall. Though Swift gave up the more
visual, more typical, less "poetic" word, he returned to it
a few years later, when he had decided to write only like himself, with

> The tortoise thus, with motion slow,
> Will clamber up a wall....
> ("To the Rev. Mr. Daniel Jackson,"
>   37-38)

He knew that neither Addison's vocabulary nor anyone else's
was like his own in which he intentionally wrote on "simple
topicks told in rime," using the plain, live, right word.

5.

SPECIFIC PARODIES

Oftener than most writers Swift intends to surprise through
his verses and epigrams, pulling the chair out from under the
inattentive or unsuspecting reader. He surprises the reader
more insidiously, less abruptly, by the trick of parody. His
scorn for cant and his love for satire were congenital, and
especially when the cant was poetic he could not resist a
rhymed parody to scotch the humbug and uncover the insin-

In antient Time, as Story tells
The Saints would often leave their Cells
And Strole about, but hide their Quality,
To try the People's Hospitality.
  It happen'd on a Winter's night
As Authors of the Legend write
Two Brother-Hermits, Saints by Trade
Taking their Tour in Masquerade
Came to a Village hard by Rixham
Ragged and not a Groat betwixt 'em.
It rain'd as hard as it could pour,
Yet they were forc't to walk an Hour
From House to House, wett to the Skin
Before one soul would let 'em in.
  They call'd at ev'ry Dore; Good People,
My Comrade's Blind, and I'm a Creeple
Here we ly Starving in the Street
T'would grieve a Body's Heart to see't.
No Christian would turn out a Beast
In such a dreadfull Night at least;
Give us but Straw, and let us Ly
In yonder Barn to keep us dry.
Thus in thes Strolers usuall Cant
They beg'd Relief which none would grant.

No

cerity of its poetical gewgaws in the light of satire. In this attempt he wielded high burlesque to fight, more relentlessly than any other important figure in English literature, the "romantic" view of poetry. It is hard to understand why Dr. Johnson found so little to approve in Swift's verses; for they take pains to ridicule the mythological imagery, unconvincing shepherds, and fatuous colloquies that the Doctor deplored in Milton's "Lycidas" and elsewhere. What Dr. Johnson only complained of, Swift lambasted: *his* weapon of complaint against such a pastoral vacuum, emptily imitated by poets after Milton, was that of extreme parody in a series of verses.

The parody was deserved. When Thomas Flatman, for instance, wrote of his own son's death, he could not honestly mourn in poetry, but attitudinized with cries of:

> Alexis! dear Alexis! lovely boy!
> O my Damon! O Palaemon! snatch'd away...

Through the enameled meadows of Flatman's poems wander "bright" Castabella, "poor" Celia, Strephon who was "the wonder of the plains," "dear" Castara, and other lovely nymphs and sexy shepherds whose names might have come from labels on bottles of cough-syrup. In one of his pastoral dialogues Flatman's lovely Parthenia inquires, with ingenuousness one does not meet again until Wordsworth's peasants begin asking questions, what is meant by death. When Castara is reluctant to tell her the cruel truth, Parthenia winningly persuades to be told it, and having heard, exclaims:

> Alas! Why will they use me so,
> A virgin that no evil do?

Flatman's odes annoyed the Earl of Rochester, who in satirical ways preceded Swift, into calling their author "that slow drudge." One of Rochester's own songs begins unprettily, "Fair Chloris in a pig-sty lay." It is easy to imagine how much more annoyed than Rochester Swift was at reading of etherial Parthenias and Celias. He had seen nothing like them in Dublin or London or anywhere else in real life, doubted that anyone else had, and objected to their interminable poetic

rendezvous. He set out to remind the world of what human
beings are really like:

> Or should a porter make enquiries
> For Chloe, Sylvia, Phillis, Iris;
> Be told the lodging, lane, and sign,
> The bow'rs that hold those nymphs divine;
> Fair Chloe would perhaps be found
> With footmen tippling under ground;
> The charming Sylvia beating flax,
> Her shoulders mark'd with bloody tracks;
> Bright Phillis mending ragged smocks;
> And radiant Iris in the pox.
>
> These are the goddesses enroll'd
> In Curll's Collections, new and old,
> Whose scoundrel fathers would not know 'em,
> If they should meet 'em in a poem.
>> ("To Stella, Who Collected and Trans-
>> cribed His Poems," 39-52)

Swift made certain that these young ladies, no longer arti-
ficially "fair," "charming," "bright," and "radiant," should
be met in poetry. If the reader is disarmed by the prepossessing title of "A Beautiful Young Nymph Going to Bed. Written
for the Honour of the Fair Sex," 1731, he is warned of parody
by the second line of the poem, where a single negative makes
the difference:

> Corinna, pride of Drury-Lane,
> For whom no shepherd sighs in vain;
>> (1-2)

but the reader is hardly prepared for the dreadful disrobing
that follows, revealing Corinna as a prostitute ravaged by
disease and bad dreams. And although we are charmingly
told of the heroine in "Strephon and Chloe," 1731, that

> So beautiful a nymph appears
> But once in twenty thousand years,
>> (3-4)

the proof of her loveliness is somewhat unconventional: she

> Would so discreetly things dispose,
> None ever saw her pluck a rose.
> Her dearest comrades never caught her
> Squat on her hams, to make maid's water.
>
> (15-18)

That is surprising and witty parody of the nymphs of poetry
whose only necessity in life is to charm sighs from an inex-
haustible retinue of shepherds whose only necessity, in turn,
is to be charmed, and whose sheep, if there were enough to
go around, must certainly have wandered from the enameled
plains and perished.

In Swift's "Pastoral Dialogue," 1729, there are no cries of
"O my Damon" nor any Celadon's whimper of "I faint, I gasp,
I pant, my eyes are set." Though they speak hilariously within the established pattern for pastoral dialogues, Swift's Der-
mot and Sheela, digging weeds, are realistically rural in
appearance, ways, and speech. They declare their love and
jealousy in talk of a shared crust and tobacco-plug, torn
breeches, and kisses stolen behind a ditch. There are surprising contrasts like that when the innocently poetic line
"Sharp are the stones, take thou this rushy mat" is followed
by a flatly unpoetic explanation of the offer: "The hardest
bum will bruise with sitting squat."

SHEELAH

> When you with Oonah stood behind a ditch,
> I peept, and saw you kiss the dirty bitch.
> Dermot, how could you touch those nasty sluts!
> I almost wisht this spud were in your guts.

DERMOT

> If Oonah once I kiss'd, forbear to chide:
> Her aunt's my gossip by my father's side:
> But, if I ever touch her lips again,
> May I be doom'd for life to weed in rain.

. . .

O, could I earn for thee, my lovely lass,
A pair of brogues to bear thee dry to Mass!
But see, where Norah with the sowins comes—
Then let us rise, and rest our weary bums.
                                (37-44, 49-52)

"Dirty bitch," "guts," and "weed in rain" are substituted
for "sly charmer," "heart," and "woo in vain" from the kind
of dialogue Swift is ridiculing. The change of the single last
word in the final line, from "Then let us rise, and rest our
weary LIMBS," caps the wit of the parody.

Herbert Davis has pointed out the same effect at the conclusion of one of Swift's lampoons on Marlborough, "A Satirical Elegy on the Death of a Late Famous General," 1722.
"It begins," Mr. Davis says, "so quietly, with a sneer that
is hardly perceptible, proceeds with a few crude jokes, as
though the subject were worth no serious consideration, and
ends with a sort of dismissal as complete as it is devas-
tating...":

His Grace! impossible! what dead!
Of old age too, and in his bed!
And could that Mighty Warrior fall?
And so inglorious, after all!
Well, since he's gone, no matter how,
The last loud trump must wake him now:
And, trust me, as the noise grows stronger,
He'd wish to sleep a little longer.
And could he be indeed so old
As by the news-papers we're told?
Threescore, I think, is pretty high;
'Twas time in conscience he should die.
                    . . .
Let pride be taught by this rebuke,
How very mean a thing's a Duke;
From all his ill-got honours flung,
Turn'd to that dirt from whence he sprung.
                                (1-12, 29-32)

Substitute "earthly honours" and "to that dust," Mr. Davis suggests, and the final lines are conventionally elegiac, and hackneyed. But Swift's parody is insidious as well as witty. It not only expresses distaste for Marlborough, makes a criticism of vainglory, and shows a scorn for a certain fashion in literature, but through honest realism it makes pompous cant phrases forever absurd, just as a caricature can wickedly make a face forever laughable. Contrasted with Swift's "Satirical Elegy," Tennyson's "Ode on the Death of the Duke of Wellington" seems a little embarrassing, however sincerely felt that poem may have been. Read alongside Swift's "Turn'd to that dirt from whence he sprung," Thomas Flatman's epitaph on the Earl of Sandwich seems unctuous and insincere in phrases like "dust of that illustrious man," "nobly courted death," and "Sandwich the Good, the Great, the Brave."

For the most part Swift seems to have had only types rather than specific poems in mind when he wrote his burlesques. One of his rhymed attacks on Richard Tighe, however, is a line-for-line parody of the poem "Clad All in White," by Cowley, whom Swift had once seriously wished to imitate. Now, in "Clad All in Brown," 1728, he imitates only to make a vicious caricature of what in his youth seemed beautiful. In six stanzas that had sung amorously of a mistress' fair charms, he changes pretty into coarse, with a vocabulary of "stink," "brute," "mud," "turds," "foulness," "filth," and "bawds."

From CLAD ALL IN WHITE	From CLAD ALL IN BROWN
Fairest thing that shines below,	Foulest brute that stinks below,
Why in this robe dost thou appear?	Why in this brown dost thou appear?
Wouldst thou a white most perfect show,	For, would'st thou make a fouler show,
Thou must at all no garment wear:	Thou must go naked all the year.
Thou wilt then seem much whiter so,	Fresh from the mud a wallowing sow
Than winter when 'tis cold with snow.	Would then be not so brown as thou.

(1-6)

Like the clever and cruel political caricatures of Gillray, this parody is meant to vex its subject at whatever cost to niceties. Like Gillray's political cartoons with which public figures were later mercilessly bombarded, "Clad All in Brown" was only one of the libelous insults with which Swift vexed his enemy Richard Tighe.

Swift's most perfect parody in verse, whose melodious lines are a pastiche of ready-made, high-toned phrases, is "A Love Song, in the Modern Taste," 1733. All its "harmonious numbers," "soft Elysian plains," and "dying vows," adapted from Ovid, are soothingly fitted together to make almost no sense at all. Swift, the great admirer of naturalness and common sense, fixes a Cupid here, a Cynthia there, to create the familiar sound of conventional love verse but carefully goes no further than sound. He observes in his first stanza that Art is here usurping the place of Nature (or Nature realized through Ovid). It is Art in the vacuous taste that annoyed him into writing parody:

> Flutt'ring spread thy purple pinions,
>   Gentle Cupid o'er my heart;
> I a slave to thy dominions;
>   Nature must give way to Art.
>
> Mild Arcadians, ever blooming,
>   Nightly nodding o'er your flocks,
> See my weary days consuming,
>   All beneath yon flow'ry rocks.
>   . . .
> Melancholly smooth Meander,
>   Swiftly purling in a round,
> On thy margin lovers wander,
>   With thy flow'ry chaplets crown'd.
>
> Thus when Philomela drooping,
>   Softly seeks her silent mate;
> See the bird of Juno stooping.
>   Melody resigns to Fate.
>   (1-8, 25-32)

Coming from the hand of Swift, "A Love Song" might be expected to bring surprise through his characteristic substitution of coarse words and phrases. The reader awaits a "bitch" or "bum" or "stink" to appear suddenly among the eight flowery stanzas; but the surprise this time comes instead from the poem's never rising, never shifting from its sweet, silly melody. And "Melody," the verses conclude, if there is a conclusion, "resigns to Fate."*

Just as his "Love Song" wittily criticizes the sublimity-without-sense that seemed to be the fate of honest poetry, so "A Cantata" burlesques what Swift felt was wrong with music in the Augustan Age. "The town is running mad after a new opera," he once wrote to Ambrose Philips. "Poetry and good sense are dwindling like echo with repetition and voice... A good old lady five miles out of town asked me the other day what these *uproars* were that her daughter was always going to." It was a time of operas, choruses, and choirs: everybody sang, as Hogarth shows in his engraving of the indignant musician outside whose window the entire town is making music, even the chimney-sweep singing in his chimney. It was a time of long-winded cantatas and Italianate songs whose words grandiloquently and repetitiously sought to imitate musical notes rather than make good sense. So Swift wrote words for a cantata in which the operatic eunuchs, prima donnas, or neighborhood chorus might hold their long notes, rush excitedly through staccato phrases, trill, soar, warble, and be free of the encumbrance of meaning. It concludes:

> See, See. . . . Ce-lia, Ce-lia
> Dies, dies, dies, dies, dies, dies, dies, dies,
> While true lov-ers.............eyes

*It has not hitherto been noted that these final stanzas resemble lines from Pope, to whom the poem has sometimes been attributed:

> Thus on Meander's flow'ry margin lies
> The expiring swan, and as he sings he dies.
>   (*The Rape of the Lock*, V, 65-66)

Weep-ing sleep, sleep-ing weep, weep-ing sleep. (Slow)
Bo peep, bo peep, bo peep, bo peep, peep, bo bo peep.
                                                    (Fast)

Thomas Arne, the talented composer of settings for texts
from Milton and Shakespeare, as well as for Thomson's "Rule
Britannia," wanted to set music to this cantata-to-end-can-
tatas; and Faulkner, Swift's publisher in Dublin, hoped it
would "run more than the Beggar's Opera...." But when
Faulkner printed it with music by the Rev. John Echlin the
year after Swift's death, there was no such success.

Swift himself had suggested Gay's writing the "Newgate
pastoral, among the whores and thieves there," that became
the most famous musical parody of its kind, laughing the
opera-singing Italians back into the wings of the stage. When
tunes from *The Beggar's Opera* were sung everywhere in London, and even in Dublin, Swift wrote to Gay to inquire especially about the popularity of the song beginning "When
you censure the age." That song and two others, beginning
"Through all the employments of life" and "Since laws were
made for ev'ry degree," have sometimes been credited to
Swift, who may at least have made suggestions for them.

6.

"THE LEGION CLUB"

One of Swift's poems growing from indignant comment upon
topical events holds critical respect as a diatribe almost un-
equaled in the literature of the world. Characterized as the
bitterest of his philippics, most terrible of his satires, and a
nightmare of "black fire and horror," "The Legion Club,"
1736, seems never to have been read without a measure of
awe, Dr. Delany going so far as to think it Swift's greatest
accomplishment in verse. It expresses his acrimonious contempt for the Irish Parliament he named the Legion Club after
the Unclean Spirit that answered: "My name is Legion: for we
are many." In jest that was not wholly playful Swift had
written to his friend Lord Orrery that rather than keep com-

pany with his Lordship who had just come "reeking from that
abominable Club," he would leave Dublin; and to Sheridan he
wrote: "The Club meets in a week, and I determine to leave
the town as soon as possible, for I am not able to live with
the air of such rascals...." Early in 1736, when the House
of Commons, by resolution, favored the cattle-grazers' wish
to be rid of tithes from which the clergy benefited, Swift expressed his accumulated resentment. Fulfilling through rhyme
his wish for violent action, he would have the Irish Parliament
House blasted by the devil and all the "rascals" shut in cells
like gibbering madmen.

The opening lines are casually and disarmingly good-natured,
with a humorous rhyme of "oft I" and "lofty," a half-told jest,
a description of the Parliament House, and no suggestion of
the unleashed invective to follow. But when the question of
the ninth line —"Tell us, what this pile contains?"—receives
an answer, the invective, though still only snarling, begins.
It snaps and bites by the time Swift puts the "abominable
Club" in a place for lunatics and goes to watch them, each

> With a passage left to creep in
> And a hole above for peeping.
>   (45-46)

Lending elevation of phrase, for contrast and juxtaposition of
styles, the *Aeneid* is imitated:

> All ye gods, who rule the soul
> Styx, through Hell whose waters roll!
> Let me be allow'd to tell
> What I heard in yonder Hell.
>
> Near the door an entrance gapes,
> Crouded round with antic shapes;
> Poverty, and Grief, and Care,
> Causeless Joy, and true Despair;
> Discord periwigg'd with snakes,
> See the dreadful strides she takes.
>   (83-92)

But the borrowed Latin Hell soon gives way to an eighteenth-
century English Bedlam in which Swift now converses matter-
of-factly and characteristically with the keeper, as though on
a dreadful and fantastic sightseeing jaunt. He observes fourteen of the "rascals" as they "sit a picking straws" and
"dabble in their dung." Alongside these manifestations of
lunacy Swift shows himself, representing the rational world,
casually tipping the keeper, making interested inquiries, and
taking snuff as he watches the madmen.

> When I saw the Keeper frown,
> Tipping him with half a crown;
> Now, said I, we are alone,
> Name your heroes, one by one.
>
>   . . .
>
> Keeper, shew me where to fix
> On the puppy pair of Dicks;
> By their lanthorn jaws and leathern,
> You might swear they both are brethren:
> Dick Fitz-Baker, Dick the Player,
> Old acquaintance, are you there?
> Dear companions hug and kiss,
> Toast old Glorious in your piss.
> Tye them Keeper in a tether,
> Let them stare and stink together;
> Both are apt to be unruly,
> Lash them daily, lash them duly,
> Though 'tis hopeless to reclaim them,
> Scorpion rods perhaps may tame them.
>   (133-136, 145-158)

Critics who have called "The Legion Club" a nightmare of
demoniac horror have had in mind the cumulative effect of its
railing abuse. The effect is a conscious one: lines like "Lash
them daily, lash them duly," for instance, perform exactly,
through meter and sound, what Swift intended of them. And he
turns from violence to elegant malice:

> Keeper, I must now retire,
> You have done what I desire:

> But I feel my spirits spent,
> With the noise, the sight, the scent.
>
> Pray be patient, you shall find
> Half the best are still behind:
> You have hardly seen a score,
> I can shew two hundred more.
>
> Keeper, I have seen enough,
> Taking then a pinch of snuff;
> I concluded, looking round 'em,
> May their God, the Devil confound 'em.
>   (231-242)

"I have written a very masterly poem on the Legion Club,"
Swift wrote, "which, if the printer will be condemned to be
hanged for it, you will see in a three-penny book..." For
him, its effectiveness lay partly in the fact that it was a libelous, hanging matter. Alfred Lord Tennyson, his son has
recorded, "was greatly impressed by the deadly earnest and
savagery, and let me say *sadness* of Swift's 'Legion Club.'
He has more than once read it to me..." For Tennyson the
metrical devices, the drama, the power of feeling, the deadly
earnestness, the paradox, and the tragic irony in the poem
would have been of interest; but the "sadness," one is in-
clined to think, he read into it from Victorian elegies.
    Perhaps the real surprise in "The Legion Club," as in
Swift's other political lampoons, springs out of the expert,
appropriate expression of an essentially prosaic content. This
effect is even more surprising in his quieter poems that do not
try so desperately, for whatever reason, to shame and irritate
and call names. When Swift wrote on "simple topicks told in
rime," applying the language of prose to verse, he was still
the great master of wit. In *A Critical History of English
Poetry* Grierson and Smith find surprise in the effect of wit
that comes from Swift's straightforward, sensible prose admirably presented as verse. They perhaps have in mind the
wonderful conversational poems, the homely poems to Stella
that could serve as models for all sincere statements of af-

fection, and Swift's self-conscious poems on himself. Actually, of course, as we have seen and shall further see, what appears to be "straightforward" in his verse, and in his prose, is very often an intentional half-truth, cold irony, or the most walloping kind of parody.

Sometimes Swift's urgent wish to describe the ridiculous or vile made his strongest verse seem to him too ineffectual and blind for his purpose, and he wanted the added power of visual vexation like that in Hogarth's later caricatures of Wilkes and Charles Churchill. Toward the end of "The Legion Club," when he had vilified, abused, and denounced the men he hated, Swift expressed this wish for assistance in his wit:

> How I want thee, humorous Hogart?
> Thou I hear, a pleasant rogue art;
> Were but you and I acquainted,
> Every monster should be painted;
> You should try your graving tools
> On this odious group of fools;
> Draw the beasts as I describe 'em,
> Form their features, while I gibe them;
> Draw them like, for I assure you,
> You will need no *car'catura:*
> Draw them so that we may trace
> All the soul in every face.
>   (219-230)

Though Hogarth preferred "characters" to "*caricaturas*," he shared Swift's wish to reform by any means, protesting the excesses of contemporary Dutch art, for example, by public laughter, ridicule, and by parodies "scratched in the true Dutch taste." Both the artist and the poet for their purposes sometimes depicted vulgar life in which the depraved mother pours gin down her infant's throat, the politicians are maudlin-drunk, the old man makes water against a wall, and Justice is a blowzy goddess with only one eye covered. They used, too, for their purposes the surprise of juxtaposition wherein the powdered and beribboned fop stands in the street with his toe almost touching the dead, decaying cat.

We do not nowadays deplore the invention and surprise in Hogarth's engravings, but instead praise them for their wit and genius. In Swift's poems of wit—"The Day of Judgement," "A Description of a City Shower," "Baucis and Philemon," "The Legion Club," and perhaps even some others that are almost forgotten—there is an analogous show of genius that waits for general praise.

CHAPTER FOUR

HE RECONCIL'D DIVINITY AND WIT

1.

MORAL POEMS

To vex the whole world was Swift's intention. Poetic variety, wicked wit, and the horse-laugh and dry rub of humor were useful implements in the hands of this churchman and reformer, who meant to persuade, scold, and preach against corruption:

> From the planet of my birth,
> I encounter vice with mirth.
>
> - - -
>
> As my method of reforming
> Is by laughing, not by storming...
> ("Epistle to a Lady," 141-142, 229-230)

He could spend his rage in a jest, he said, and the jest more likely than a serious sermon might assist in driving out mankind's hypocrisy and hate. Righteously indignant rather than cheaply cynical or sadistic, he thought wit the most effective way to express his indignation: the lash for him was more persuasive than the cudgel. In his life-long earnest attempt

to expose vice and folly, he recognized his similarity to
Latin satirists who knew the power of the ridiculous:

> It is well observed by Horace,
> Ridicule has greater pow'r
> To reform the world, than sour.
> ("Epistle to a Lady," 198-200)

And so in many of his poems he sought through laughter to
call the age's attention to its ills, using wit to shock mankind into sanity, often distorting in a furious, grotesque fashion meant to remind the sick world of its own distortions.

The incorporation of divinity and wit is masterly in Swift's
prose pieces like "An Argument to Prove that the Abolishing
of Christianity in England May, as Things Now Stand, Be At-
tended with Some Inconveniences, and Perhaps not Produce
Those Many Good Effects Proposed Thereby." Their foolery
has a grave and earnest purpose. Using verse, Swift similarly
delivers a sermon with an appended moral in the witty "Beasts
Confession to the Priest," 1732, which carries the subtitle
"On Observing How Most Men Mistake Their Own Talents."
Like an old beast-fable it draws a parallel between talking
animals and men to show our universal folly of admitting only
to faults that are virtues in excess. Ironic lines that slyly
comment on hypocrisy in religion introduce the fable:

> When beasts could speak (the learned say
> They still can do so every day)
> It seems they had religion then,
> As much as now we find in men.
> (1-4)

Commanded to confess their sins, the wolf admits that he
has innocently broken his fast; the ass confesses himself a
wit; the swine is over-proud of his shape and beauty; the
ape is a stoic; and the goat explains his chastity. Among
men, likewise, the lawyer insists he has never squeezed a
needy client; the knave who seeks a place pretends he cannot
flatter; the chaplain trusts only to merit for promotion; the

doctor is too altruistic; the card-sharper is never a winner;
and

> The statesman tells you with a sneer,
> His fault is to be too sincere;
> And, having no sinister ends,
> Is apt to disoblige his friends.
>
> . . .
>
> He thought it base for men in stations,
> To crowd the court with their relations:
> His country was his dearest mother,
> And ev'ry virtuous man his brother...
> (141-144, 177-180)

In those mocking lines Swift writes with more power and
persuasion than when he occasionally seeks to be as homi-
letic as any poet concerned less with wit than with a moral.
But even when his subject is "The Birth of Manly Virtue,
from Callimachus," 1725, he turns it into a pleasant tribute
to Lord Carteret; his "Desire and Possession," 1727, is the
fairly exciting allegory of brothers who both perish in their
race toward Fortune; and "On Censure," 1721, like some of
his greater poems, drops suddenly in its final couplet from an
impersonal discussion of "detracting people" to a personal
and colloquial solution:

> The most effectual way to baulk
> Their malice, is——to let them talk.
> (29-30)

Swift's sermons, miscellaneous writings on religion, and
"moral" verses are often in a style deceptively proper and
plain. Another poet-preacher, John Donne, had composed both
his sermons and poems from subtle conceits and knotted loops
of rhetoric. In prayers and sacred hymns he played with puns
even more rudely forced than those in his love-poems. Now, a
century later, Swift's sermon "On the Causes of the Wretched
Condition of Ireland," for instance, or his sermon "On Doing
Good," deals with problems of the day in plain language intended to touch the common sense of its most ignorant hearer.

THE SIN OF WIT

Indeed, in his "Letter to a Young Gentleman Lately Enter'd into Holy Orders," Swift warns against the old seventeenth-century wit based upon style:

> I cannot forbear warning you in the most earnest man-ner against endeavouring at wit in your sermons, because by the strictest computation, it is very near a million to one that you have none; and because too many of your calling have consequently made themselves everlastingly ridiculous by attempting it. I remember several young men in this town, who could never leave the pulpit under half a dozen conceits; and this faculty adhered to those gentlemen a longer or shorter time exactly in proportion to their several degrees of dulness; accordingly, I am told that some of them retain it to this day. I heartily wish the brood were at an end.

In this "Letter to a Young Gentleman" first appeared the renowned phrase that Dr. Johnson applied to Swift's poems; "Proper words in proper places," Swift tells the Young Gentleman, "make the true definition of a style." He goes on to advise against obscurities, ambiguities, and vagrant emotion in the pulpit, where the simple purpose of a sermon should not be to spellbind but to tell people their duty and then convince them of its truth. Do not attempt to explain religious mysteries, he warns the Young Gentleman: for, once explained, they are mysteries no longer. Do not waste breath in preaching against atheism, he adds: for atheists will not be in the church to hear, and it is foolhardy to proffer doubts that churchgoers may find attractive.

Swift's own sermons and "didactic" poems—they could hardly, like Donne's, be called "divine"—are seldom so simple and proper as they pretend. They can be as ironical as the "Argument against Abolishing Christianity" or as mocking as the "abstract" of Anthony Collins's "Discourse of Free Thinking," purportedly put into "plain English... for the use of the poor." They borrow the "bite" of Jove on Judgment Day, use *la bagatelle* for purposes of divinity, and draw a moral from the foolish bric-a-brac of a coquette's mind. They bring the force of wit through irony and paradox and shock.

2.

"UNPRINTABLE" POEMS

Shock alone, however, has been the reaction to certain of
his poems. Though shocking literature, if it really is literature,
has a way of turning respectable with time, and what censors
frown upon in one age may in another be memorized by school-
boys for their teachers, after two centuries there are certain
poems by Jonathan Swift that are embarrassing to scholars,
shunned by anthologists, and unknown to almost everyone
else. Even the most dispassionate modern critics have called
these poems nasty, noxious, disgusting, and painful, and have
hastened past with eyes averted. "Strephon and Chloe,"
1731, describing a wedding night, seems especially to have
frightened readers with its casual talk of armpits and toes.
It is otherwise hard to understand why the poem has not been
recognized as one of the wittiest and one of the most serious
of all Swift's efforts. Its surprises are thick-coming and varied.
Parody in the poem is first suggested by the borrowed, pastoral names of the bridal pair; but even with "hampers full of
bleeding hearts" and "infant Loves with purple wings," the
parody would not surprise without Swiftian lines like

> . . . pigeons billing, sparrows treading,
> Fair emblems of a fruitful wedding.

and

> The rites perform'd, the parson paid,
> In state return'd the grand parade . . .
> (51-52, 67-68)

Here the humorous joining of formal and colloquial serves
as the motif for the whole poem: this is Strephon's story of
how he idealized his bride as a deity only to discover her a
human animal like him, his poetic dream becoming as much a
down-to-earth reality as the shameless sparrows and the fee
for the parson. At first poor Strephon, perplexed and embar-

rassed in his nightcap, does not know how to approach his
bride:

> The weather and his love were hot:

but

> Can such a deity endure
> A mortal human touch impure?
> How did the humbled swain detest
> His prickled beard, and hairy breast!
> His night-cap border'd round with lace
> Could give no softness to his face.
>
> (81, 89-94)

To reassure himself he reflects that "A certain goddess, God
knows who," once bestowed love on mortal man; and he has
hopes. But his Chloe, unlike the goddess, is unreceptive—
for a very human reason that Swift expresses in an elegant
couplet. Incredulous, Strephon becomes aware that his celes-
tial nymph (who has drunk twelve cups of tea) "brings a
vessel into bed":

> Carminative and diuretick,
> Will damp all passion sympathetick...
>   . . .
> But, soon with like occasions prest,
> He boldly sent his hand in quest,
> (Inspir'd with courage from his bride)
> To reach the pot on t'other side.
> And as he fill'd the reeking vase,
> Let fly a rouzer in her face.
>
> The little Cupids hov'ring round,
> (As pictures prove) with garlands crown'd,
> Abasht at what they saw and heard,
> Flew off, nor evermore appear'd.
>
> (133-134, 187-196)

Though he may cling fast to the idea that certain subjects
are not allowed in poetry, the modern reader will recognize
that the first-quoted couplet, with its "Carminative and diu-
retick," would grace the polysyllabic "Mr. Eliot's Sunday

Morning Service." But while there are calloused feet, sweat,
and dirty hands in the poetry of T.S. Eliot, there is no
"rouzer." The surprise of the line in which that word appears,
startling the reader to laughter or at least to exclamation,
dispels the parody of pastoral verse. Immediately, then, Swift
shows cupids in flight; and from the unreal, disappointing
world of pretty pictures, Strephon and his Chloe change to
one still more disappointing. They accept, Swift says, a
coarse world without beauty, decency, or concern for opinion;
and they "learn to call a spade a spade." For Swift the relationship characterized by Strephon's sudden rouzer is even
more offensive than hypocritical pretense of otherworldliness.
For over a hundred lines he earnestly draws his moral from the
story: marriage should be built of enduring materials, he says:
and, because beauty and youth are fleeting, they are not suf-
ficient:

> On sense and wit your passion found,
> By decency cemented round;
> Let prudence and good nature strive,
> To keep esteem and love alive.
> Then, come old age whene'er it will,
> Your friendship shall continue still:
> And thus a mutual gentle fire,
> Shall never but with life expire.
>
> (307-314)

Here the Dean of St. Patrick's Cathedral, hoping he has
prodded his reader into awareness and startled him into attention, confronts him with a sermon of wise advice. Sense and
wit, he wrote more than once in moral earnestness, are the
best foundation for a way of life. "I have been only a man of
rhymes," he said in a letter, "... yet never without a moral
view"; it was a view that commended Stella, whom he respected most among women, for her "fund of wit and sense"
and found Vanessa, as a "nymph of wit and sense," pleasing
to his eye. When it is read alongside conventionally naughty
songs of the period, in which the institution of marriage itself is kicked at, Swift's poem seems obviously didactic and
"moral" in purpose.

Like "Strephon and Chloe," Swift's earlier poem called
"The Progress of Marriage," 1722, presents the case of a
husband and wife who share no "mutual gentle fire." It depicts the contempt of a young coquette for her older husband
and concludes with Swift's vindictive expression of contempt
for the coquette, soon widowed. Lacking either wit or sense,
their empty marriage provides an entertaining subject from
which to draw a serious moral observation:

> Her spouse desires his coffee soon,
> She rises to her tea at noon...
> And drops him at the church, to pray
> While she drives on to see the play...
> (He) goes alone to take his rest
> In bed, where he can spare her best.

They have

> No common ligament that binds
> The various textures of their minds,
> Their thoughts, and actions, hopes, and fears,
> Less corresponding than their years.
>   (37-38, 81-82, 89-90, 33-36)

"The Progress of Marriage" and "Strephon and Chloe"
show admirably how Swift reconciled divinity and wit. Perhaps not so clinically interesting as the nineteenth-century
idea of a mad, disgusting Swift, the idea of a moralist and
reformer is nevertheless the truer one. It is nothing new. Dr.
Delany described his friend's poems as "prescriptions of an
able physician, who had, in truth, the health of his patients
at heart, but laboured to attain that end, not only by strong
emetics, but also, by all the most nauseous, and offensive
drugs, and potions, that could be administered." Recent
studies by Quintana and Davis have stressed the element of
moral satire in much that Swift wrote, especially in the fourth
book of *Gulliver's Travels* that is so often frowned upon, the
cold-blooded *Modest Proposal*, and the "unprintable" poems.
An earnest call to the conscience of the world, to be heard
in those works, is sounded explicitly in the epitaph Swift

wrote for his tomb in St. Patrick's Cathedral. The "saeva indignatio" of that epitaph is quoted frequently enough, but there is more to it:

> ABI, VIATOR,
> ET IMITARE, SI POTERIS,
> STRENUUM PRO VIRILI LIBER—
> TATIS VINDICEM.

A dean's appeal for us to serve human liberty has not stuck in the mind like his hairy Yahoos, servings of infants' flesh, and women in their dressing-rooms. Because he sometimes chose these subjects, Swift's name has been pinned to anonymous rhymes, like "The Art of Wenching," that had only coarseness of their own and needed his name to lend them wit.

3.

"THE LADY'S DRESSING-ROOM"

Women in their dressing-rooms were for Swift a symbol of mankind's vanity, hypocrisy, and imperfection. With this symbol he at times merely amused himself and at other times suggested a moral as T.S. Eliot does with his bored typist who accepts love on her divan. Although Eliot provides a Swiftian inventory of undergarments and dressing-room paraphernalia, he is restrained from stepping into his poem with a plain statement of distaste like Swift's:

Who sees, will spew; who smells, be poison'd.

That is the concluding line to "A Beautiful Young Nymph Going to Bed," but it could serve as well to conclude "The Lady's Dressing-Room," "The Progress of Beauty," or "Cassinus and Peter." In each there is the poetic counter-

part to Captain Lemuel Gulliver's displeasure at what he
saw and smelled in the apartments of the gigantic maids of
honor in Brobdingnag:

> For, they would strip themselves to the skin, and put on
> their smocks in my presence, while I was placed on their
> toylet directly before their naked bodies; which, I am
> sure, to me was very far from being a tempting sight, or
> from giving me any other (e)motions than those of horror
> and disgust. Their skins appeared so coarse and uneven,
> so variously coloured when I saw them near, with a mole
> here and there as broad as a trencher, and hairs hanging
> from it thicker than pack-threads; to say nothing further
> concerning the rest of their persons. Neither did they at
> all scruple while I was by, to discharge what they had
> drunk, to the quantity of at least two hogsheads, in a
> vessel that held above three tuns.

In all commentaries, observations, and essays on *Gulliver's
Travels*, though there is complaint about the indignity of
Swift's coarseness in naming nakedness and excretory pro-
cesses, there is no misunderstanding of his serious intention
to deflate human pride and folly. Brobdingnagian maidens
were charming companions to their Brobdingnagian friends,
but they were human; being human, they were imperfect. A
misanthrope, perhaps, Swift nevertheless had enough faith in
human beings to try, even by trick and jest and shock, to reform that imperfection.

In "A Beautiful Young Nymph," 1731, he describes the
wages of sin as effectively as a preacher shouting hell-fire
and brimstone, or the photographs in a medical treatise, or
the scenes drawn by Hogarth for "A Harlot's Progress." The
rather obtrusive moral affixed to Moll Hackabout's disintegration and punishment as Hogarth draws her, when she is
revealed as a hopelessly miserable creature in miserable sur-
roundings, is the moral Swift affixes to the picture of Corinna
going to bed. She is a "batter'd, strolling toast" of London
streets. There is the fascination here of sordid detail like
Hogarth's in the exact setting down of hideous wig, littered
room, and despair as Corinna returns to her bed at midnight

to remove daubed paint, artificial hair and eyebrows, glass
eye, teeth, cheek-plumpers, breast-props, corsets, and bol-
sters—unlacing, pulling, and untwisting to be free of them one
by one, like magicians' properties. This is not sufficiently
unattractive for Swift's purpose. The reader is spared nothing:

> With gentlest touch, she next explores
> Her shankers, issues, running sores,
> Effects of many a sad disaster;
> And then to each applies a plaister.
>   (29-32)

If the harlot dreams, it is tormentedly and fitfully of prison,
deportation, watchmen, constables, and bullies. Imagining
she feels the whip-lash, she screams in her sleep.

   "The Lady's Dressing-Room," 1730, is more dreadful
still. Swift's eighteenth-century acquaintance Mrs. Pilkington
recorded that her old mother threw up her dinner when she
read the poem; and that has been almost the reaction of persons as varied as James Russell Lowell, Hippolyte Taine,
and Aldous Huxley, though their explanations of the reaction
are also varied. Swift's friend Lord Orrery sought to convince
himself that "The Lady's Dressing-Room" was intended as a
warning to inexperienced youth. For Taine in the next century the poem was an emotional affront that made him complain of Swift that "il a toujours le microscope en main."
Even modern writers who have the microscope of psychology
always in hand, object to the poem: though naturalistic details figure large in the writings of D.H. Lawrence and Aldous
Huxley, they both find the poem shocking, not because it
disgusts but because of its unpleasant picture of bodily func-
tions that they feel should be celebrated. Their diagnoses of
Swift are in terms of undeveloped sexual consciousness, fear
of taboo words, and infantilism (Huxley pretends to think that
a twentieth-century Swift would write not about Yahoos but
about Peter Pan); and they let the subject go with that.
   If a sensitive critic like Coleridge, a hundred years after
Swift's time, dwells upon the false misanthropy, physical
dirt, and coarseness in the writings, and if a sensible critic

J.S. Muller inv. del. et Sc.

like George Orwell, a hundred years later still, calls Swift
a diseased writer who magnifies and distorts in poems like
"A Lady's Dressing-Room," it is important to see what Swift
really says. In the first place, he is hardly more scatological
than others of his contemporaries. It is Smollett, and not
Swift, who lingers in *Adventures of an Atom* upon the subject of dunghills, scorbutic dysentery, close-stools, and the
rite of posterior-worship; and it is Prior, not Swift, whose
poem "On a Fart, Let in the House of Commons" may be
found among his other poems entitled "God is Love," "On
Exodus iii. 14," and "Charity Never Faileth." Gay and Pope,
as well as Swift, thought it amusing to write verses about
the Goddess Cloacina; and the scatological was expected in
lampoons such as those against the Puritans. With Swift, however, the subject is not always merely funny. It becomes
sometimes a serious symbol, employed when he wishes to be
most serious and compelling — in *A Tale of a Tub*, *Gulliver*,
and certain poems. It becomes a symbol like the rose, the
tower, the darkness, the sunflower, or the turning wheel important in the work of other poets. "The Queen is well,"
Swift once wrote to Stella, "but I fear will be no long liver;
for I am told she has sometimes the gout in her bowels (I hate
the word *bowels*)." Hate, obsession, and seriousness make
the symbol a disturbing and effective one when Swift writes
of the Aeolists or the Yahoos, and it is disturbingly introduced into "The Lady's Dressing-Room." It is a symbol
which perhaps better than any other reduces all mankind to
a single level. In Swift's context human excrement is defined
as the antithesis of the sublime.

When Alexander Pope described Belinda's dressing-room
in *The Rape of the Lock*, intending to mock her pretense of
divinity, he lacked Swift's singleness of purpose: there is a
delicate, dainty charm in Belinda's "Puffs, powders, patches,
Bibles, billet-doux," ivory combs, and shining rows of pins.
Celia's dressing-room as Swift depicts it in his poem is like
a room filled to the ceiling with articles from Brobdingnag,
its combs, towels, handkerchiefs, vials of ointment, tweezers,
and mirror seeming as large as tables and beds. Indeed, because tables and beds are nowhere mentioned, so far as the

reader knows the filthy washbasin and chamberpot comprise
the furniture. The mirror, suitably, is a magnifying glass:

> It shew'd the visage of a giant:
> A glass that can to sight disclose
> The smallest worm in Celia's nose...
>   (62-64)

But if all the objects in the room were seen through a magnifying glass, they could hardly be more formidable. Celia's
smock is soiled with "arm-pits well besmear'd"; there are
stains on the toes of her stockings; her handkerchief is "var-
nished o'er with snuff and snot"; her combs are filled with
a paste of "Sweat, dandriff, powder, lead and hair"; and
her towels are

> Begumm'd, bematter'd, and beslim'd;
> With dirt, and sweat, and ear-wax grim'd.
>   (45-46)

If Swift had proceeded no further with "The Lady's Dressing-Room," it would stand, with its stained garments lying
beside the beribboned synthetic silks and its stinks mixing
with the fog of perfumes, as a wholly successful antidote to
all the lovely, indigestible confections that sometimes pass
as poetry. Swift does go further. He intrudes queerly into the
poem to speak, and speaks queerly: he, rather than Celia's
dirty towels, makes the reader feel uneasy. He introduces an
ingenuous Strephon to discover the sights and smells as he
walks about the dressing-room Celia has left, and his discovery leads him to think of all women in terms of "excre-
mental smell." Professing pity for Strephon, Swift pretends
also to be patronizingly amused by the boy's queasy stomach:

> Should I the Queen of Love refuse,
> Because she rose from stinking ooze?
>   . . .
> When Celia all her glory shows,
> If Strephon would but stop his nose;
> Who now so impiously blasphemes
> Her ointments, daubs, and paints and creams,

> Her washes, slops, and every clout,
> With which he makes so foul a rout;
> He soon would learn to think like me,
> And bless his ravisht eyes to see
> Such order from confusion sprung,
> Such gaudy tulips rais'd from dung.
>   (131-132, 135-144)

In these lines the tone is somehow wrong. Is it after all one thing for a Restoration wit like the Earl of Dorset to sing "In grey hair'd Celia's wither'd arms / As nightly Lewis lay," and quite another thing for Dean Swift to attempt a similar subject in verse? He appears to have made his own stomach, like Strephon's, somewhat queasy by examination of washes and slops, so that even his Swiftian irony, when he pretends insensitive affection for the gaudy tulips of love, loses its usual force and seems to mock itself. It is as though the reformer has been convinced by his own argument and the preacher has frightened himself with his own description of Man's flaws and failings.

Although Celia of "The Progress of Beauty," 1719, makes her appearance in alternating lines of rhyme rather than in couplets and she is likened, through ingenious conceit, to the moon, she is the same untidy Celia; and her Strephon is as easily bamboozled by outward appearances:

> To see her from her pillow rise
> All reeking in a cloudy steam,
> Crackt lips, foul teeth, and gummy eyes,
> Poor Strephon, how would he blaspheme!
>   (13-16)

Still a third Celia, in "Cassinus and Peter," 1731, has driven Cassinus to distraction by his discovery, like that of the Strephons, and, one might possibly add, Swift himself, that she has an alimentary canal.

While these poems were certainly written from moral and emotional compunctions that moved Swift, they were at the the same time exercises in wit, as his experiments with

certain ideas and repeated phrases show. With slight alterations and shifting of emphasis, one line appears almost iden-
tically in three different poems: in "The Lady's Dressing-
Room" it is "Oh! Celia, Celia, Celia shits!" That exclamation becomes a melancholy declaration in the last line of
"Cassinus and Peter" and an unbelieving question in "Strephon and Chloe." In its context in each poem the line is more
impressive and more shocked than shocking. It represents a
part of Swift's attempt in poetry to state one of the funda-
mental moral and emotional problems of civilized Man, though
in this it is too specialized to succeed wholly.

With less effort, apparently, though he is almost as bold,
W.B. Yeats expresses this same paradoxical idea in his
"Crazy Jane Talks with the Bishop," when he links "fair"
with "foul" and observes that the house of love lies in a
"place of excrement." Yeats, who in his later years used
Swift as a model, may very well have learned this speech, so
casually and neatly expressed, from him. But in the witty,
deadly serious, and remarkable "unprintable" poems, which
should more often be printed and read, Swift writes with a
curious insistence hardly to be encountered even in the most
"naturalistic" modern verse.

Swift's is an insistence like that of the woodcut "Cruelty
in Perfection," with which Hogarth hoped to reform the
world, showing the murdered girl with her head severed from
her body, her hand severed from her arm, and, as though that
were not enough, her finger severed from her hand. It is an
insistence necessary for a world that covers its ears or, when
it listens, turns its back. To make himself heard by persons
who complain that life is bad enough without being reminded
of it in poetry, Swift sometimes pretended to sing a ditty or
crack a joke or tell an odd little fable through which his
voice grew very impatient, very insistent, and very loud. When
his disgust shows itself, the poetry is not necessarily dis-
pelled. Disgust and insult, as Shakespeare and Swift and certain twentieth-century poets prove, are good subjects, perhaps
among the few good ones that have not been worked to death.

Modern poets have said that if verse is to become human again, it must first become brutal; that a poet may profit from the diligent study of hatred; that private disgust and scornful wit can be the stuff of excellent song; and that poetry must rub against life itself and every experience of life whether mean, or common, or speaking it out, unspeakable. J.M. Synge, Robert Graves, W.B. Yeats, T.S. Eliot, and W.H. Auden have all made this kind of statement and to some extent have demonstrated it in their poetry. Even Robert Frost, in 1946, commenting on the crude war poetry of the time, is reported as having said: "Of what I have read, the best is the more obscene."

Obscenity, if it ever appears in Swift's poetry, is not an end in itself, although the modern reader may wish that it were. Through his private disgust put to rhyme, Swift meant to ridicule the trumped-up poetry of sighing nymphs and panting shepherds; to snatch away the old fraud of Woman's simpering perfection; to reform the world's hypocrisy; and, raising his voice almost didactically, to say aloud in front of everyone that these frauds are a barrier to the life he praised: a life founded on sense and honesty and wit.

CHAPTER FIVE

SHOALS OF CRITICS

Whilst thus I write, vast shoals of critics come,
And on my verse pronounce their saucy doom...
("To Mr. Congreve," 213-214)

Within the past twenty-five years there have been published a selection from Swift's poems in handsome format, a scholarly work called *Swift's Verse: An Essay*, and the entire poetical writings in three annotated volumes that are a model of editing. It would seem that Swift has at last been made accessible and can now speak for himself as a poet, if he has anything to say. But the selection, introduced somewhat grudgingly by R. Ellis Roberts and published by the Golden Cockerel Press in 1928, is limited to only 375 copies. In *Swift's Verse: An Essay* (London, 1929) F. Elrington Ball attempts only to fix the canon of the poems. This is accomplished with far greater perspicacity in the three volumes of *The Poems of Jonathan Swift* (Oxford, 1937); Harold Williams, the editor, limits the genuine pieces to two hundred and fifty, thus dropping one hundred and fifty pieces that were conjectural, and he seeks to aid the work of other scholars by determining dates of composition, collating, and providing textual apparatus. Anyone dealing seriously with Swift, whether primarily with his poetry or not, must refer to Mr. Williams's edition. But there is still no good edition of the poems to be read as poems; and there has never been an extended consideration of what Swift was trying to do in poetry, to what degree he succeeded, and whether the poems themselves can give pleasure to a modern reader.

A few critics, and only very recently, have suggested the illumination that might come from an undismayed reading of what Swift wrote in rhyme. Ricardo Quintana in his *Mind and Art of Jonathan Swift*, 1936, ventures to defend some of the poetry against charges of triviality and ugliness. Edmund Wilson recommends it, in a brief review, as a paradoxical kind of lyric that sneers and curses while it sings. A.L. Rowse, in a similarly brief review, goes further to insist that whatever Swift accomplished in his prose he did as well in his poetry. Most notably, Herbert Davis in his study of "Swift's View of Poetry" examines the intention that lay behind the rhymed curses and sneers. All these critics, even those who offer unprecedented praise, are careful to describe the critical hurdle to be jumped and estimate its formidable height. Nobody, they remind us, has ever found sublimity in the poetry of Jonathan Swift. Hardly anyone has tried to read the poems sympathetically, separating the enduring from the dross and judging them by Swift's own critical standards.

When they first appeared, Swift's poems were popular at the booksellers', read aloud in coffeehouses, and discussed at court. Their topicality and metrical correctness were equal sources of interest. Even during Swift's lifetime, however, the poems were sometimes judged by standards he had specifically renounced. In 1728, the year Esther Johnson, "Stella," died and soon after he had begun his final self-exile in Ireland, a diatribe called *Gulliveriana* was published in an attempt to discredit the poems. The frontispiece to *Gulliveriana* shows Swift staring out upon the world. He is bewigged and wears a long gown, not sufficiently long to conceal what is unmistakably his cloven, goatish devil's foot. Aided by a lopsided Alexander Pope, he holds a volume of the *Miscellanies* aloft, over the horned head of a little satyr. In the foreground of the

engraving another satyr that must be Satan himself clasps one
hand of a posturing, parti-colored Harlequin whose other hand
is raised, thumb to nose. According to the angry author of
Gulliveriana, Swift's prose is "abominable," "bizarre,"
"wild," and "profane." But it is his poetry, quoted and imitated to prove it rubbish, that most offends:

> He cannot pretend ever to have writ any one piece, that
> can be called a poem, in the genuine sense of the word:
> No! he knew himself too well, ever to deviate out of his
> burlesque stile and manner; which is rhiming indeed, but
> nothing like poetry.... Low, groveling poetry all of it;
> and I challenge all the world, to show one good epic,
> elegiac or lyric poem of his; one eclogue, pastoral, or
> anything like the antients; and as he can't write like
> them, so they had no name for such a writer as he is:
> And his doggrel and burlesque had banish'd him Rome,
> notwithstanding he is so often huzza'd in Dublin.

The name of Jonathan Smedley, the vinegarish author of
Gulliveriana, has a kind of immortality because it is a butt
for abuse in Pope's *Dunciad* and in rhymed broadsides and
parodies by Swift. Smedley's attacks on Pope and Swift were
venomous. He wrote the notorious verses said to have been
attached to the door of St. Patrick's Cathedral and was responsible for *The Metamorphosis, A Poem, Shewing the Change of
Scriblerus into Snarlerus, Or the Canine Appetite Demonstrated
in the Persons of P-pe and Sw—t*. His invective is so crazy
that it could persuade no one. Yet in his uncritical and almost
hysterical denial of Swift as a poet, Jonathan Smedley has
the voice of others who have sometimes seen the devil's foot
beneath Swift's gown and have damned him for the sin of wit.

Within ten years after his death, Swift was the subject of
three first-hand accounts: Lord Orrery's *Remarks*, 1752; the
Rev. Patrick Delany's *Observations upon Lord Orrery's Remarks*, 1754; and Deane Swift's *Essay*, 1755. These are eval-
uations by a person of quality, a crony, and a young relative.
Somewhat condescending in his judgments, Orrery demonstrates how coarseness may be a blemish upon true genius.
Dr. Delany is loyal if uncritical in searching for Swiftian

Stella!

PA E[...]

Tantæ
Molis
erat

Me quoque Vatem

Socia
Arma
Capelle

Hoc Genus Omne

Veritas Invenit,   Justitia Sculp.

passages that may be praised for gentility and fine imagination. Deane Swift's contribution lies chiefly in his attempt
to determine accurate texts and dates of composition. All
three dwell upon the poetry at length. "Upon a general view
of his poetry," Orrery writes, "we shall find him, as in his
other performances, an uncommon, surprizing, heteroclite
genius: luxurious in his fancy, lively in his ideas, humorous
in his descriptions, and bitter, exceeding bitter in his satyr."
Here, even when he shudders slightly at the bitterness, Orrery
smiles with too much approbation upon the Dean, and he hur-
ries to add his opinion that the poems, after all, do not rise
to sublime flights of "airy motion."

A few of Swift's contemporaries recognized that he had
something other than "airy motion" in mind—something more
audacious, surprising, and witty—and commended his poetry
for the very reason that it flies in the face of the "sublime."
In June, 1750, the apostrophizing, pretty versifier William
Shenstone wrote to Lady Luxborough in praise of what his own
work lacks: he sees Swift as the poetical genius of his age,
superior to Pope, because of his "inconceivable invention"
and because he is "in a way rather contemptuous of regular
poetry and therefore manly." In 1764, from a somewhat different point of view, Goldsmith remarks upon this contempt for
"regular poetry." According to Goldsmith much of Swift's
fame stems from his boldness, his determination to draw
nature as it is, and his distaste for the "spirit of romance
mixed with all the works of the poets who preceded him."

So shrewd a reader as Dr. Johnson must surely have felt
the astonishing force of the contempt and boldness in the
poetry; but in all matters concerning Swift, Dr. Johnson was
incontrovertibly pig-headed, approving *A Tale of a Tub* only
by the supercilious observation that it must be from someone
else's pen. What might have been a brilliant evaluation, lighting the way for other critics, is instead an exercise in am-
biguity—five sentences so bland and intentionally noncom-
mittal that they become invidious. "In the poetical works of
Dr. Swift," says Dr. Johnson, "there is not much upon which
the critic can exercise his powers. They are often humorous,
almost always light, and have the qualities which recommend

such compositions, easiness and gaiety. They are, for the most part, what their author intended. The diction is correct, the numbers are smooth, and the rhymes exact. There seldom occurs a hard-laboured expression or a redundant epithet; all his verses exemplify his own definition of a good style— they consist of 'proper words in proper places.'" This is a chary description of a capable kind of poetry, but it does not show us what Swift wrote, because it stops short, as Dr. Johnson certainly intended. If the poetry had been merely correct, smooth, exact, easy, and proper, even without sublimity it would today very likely be familiar in anthologies, set to music, recited in schoolrooms, and not very interesting. Other qualities, such as the boldness, parody, and paradox in Swift's poetry, are what make it worth talking about.

After Dr. Johnson, until today, the poems have satisfied hardly anyone except Byron, who admired their rhymes, and Hazlitt, who liked their irony, satire, and sense. *The European Magazine* for November, 1790, describes them as "nothing more than prose in rhyme. Imagination, metaphor, and sublimity constitute no part of their merit. Sir Isaac Newton was within a trifle as great a poet as Dr. Swift." This is the tone of voice to which one becomes accustomed. Even Sir Walter Scott, who edited the poems, looks in vain for sublimity, saying that the appearance of grandeur in them is due to the accidental intensity of Swift's invective, and never to "sublimity either of conception or expression." For Leigh Hunt the poetry is only "a kind of smart prose." And although Thackeray can extol the sublime in Pope's *Dunciad*, he must remark upon Swift's fear of using "the poetical power which he really possessed...." "As fierce a beak and talon as ever struck—as strong a wing as ever beat, belonged to Swift," says Thackeray; but he does not associate fierceness and strength with sublimity where Swift is concerned. In America, James Russell Lowell's voice rises shrilly in condemnation of "the filthy cynicism of Swift, who delighted to uncover the nakedness of our common mother."

There is disapproval even from scholars who have connected their names with Swift. "His society verses," J. Nichol writes as an introduction to some of them, "are like

those of a man writing with his feet, for he delights to trample
on what others caress. Often he seems, among singing birds,
a vulture screeching over carrion." R. Ellis Roberts pre-
faces the poems by an admission of his own disgust, amusement and pity. More recently still, introducing his choice from
the poems, W.A. Eddy repeats the old judgment that they are
largely "not fit for reading."

All the critics, beginning with Jonathan Smedley, have been
astute in noting Swift's burlesque style and manner, his intensity of invective, and his lack of airy motion. These are
terms that he would himself have applied to the poetry. To
conclude that it is filthy cynicism, unfit for decent reading,
seems much less astute, however. And such a damning conclusion, oblivious of Swift's great wit, has worst of all en-
couraged depreciation and neglect of the poems, which are
nowadays hard to find except among the paraphernalia of
textbooks. Throughout the eighteenth century, in collections
like Vicesimus Knox's *Elegant Extracts*, Swift was gener-
ously represented. Since then his poems have faded from the
anthologies. Jonathan Swift is not represented by even a line
in Palgrave's *Golden Treasury*, Pancoast's *Standard English
Poems*, Quiller-Couch's *Oxford Book of English Verse*, or
Untermeyer's *Book of Living Verse*. As many as fifty different poems by Swift can, however, be tracked down here and
there in volumes like *The Oxford Book of Eighteenth Century
Verse*, *A Treasury of Unfamiliar Lyrics*, and *The Less-Known
British Poets*. Ralph Waldo Emerson included part of the
fierce "Day of Judgement" in his anthology called *Parnassus;*
and in *The Children's Garland from the Best Poets*, Coventry
Patmore saw fit to place Swift's "Baucis and Philemon" between "An Epitaph on a Robin Redbreast" and "Lullaby for
Titania."

Swift in the company of Robin Redbreast is rare. For two
hundred years he has displeased a certain kind of reader who
cannot admit that poetry wears different faces to suit the era,
the fashion, the mood, or the subject at hand.

But Swift's verse does deserve serious consideration alongside his prose. Like the prose of *Gulliver's Travels, A Tale*

of a Tub, and *A Modest Proposal*, the verse at its best is in
the form of parody carried to a level that transcends parody.
His wit in both verse and prose has its source primarily in
reaction. After his youthful, infelicitous experiences with
lofty numbers and second-hand sublimity, he never again
allowed himself the possibility of bursting foolishly in attempted flight. Renouncing Cowley and what had seemed
major poetry, he cleared for himself an area in which he might
be an excellent minor poet: a relatively safe area that pre-
cluded any charges of failure with the style sublime. That
repudiated style indeed provided a source for parody now in
vocabulary, images, and attitudes, contributing—when it had
been taught a new dance—an important part to Swift's area of
wit. The lofty vocabulary, images, and attitudes now laugh-
ably were made to assist in an extraordinary kind of poetry
that intended to surprise, and could shock.

In studies of Swift's career there is often a waste of critical curiosity about his turning suddenly, from his early
poetic style that did not fit his talent, to a parodying style
in which he was nearly perfect. If he had not turned, he would
not have been Jonathan Swift. And it is not indispensable to
know whether he wrote as he finally did because Dryden had
told him he would never be a poet, or because he was jealous
of Congreve, or because he admired the style of Voiture, or
because he was rebelling against the intimidations of Sir
William Temple, or because he was ashamed of common birth,
or because his sex-life was unsatisfactory, or simply because
he was improving upon the satiric tradition of Samuel Butler's *Hudibras*. None of these may be the whole truth. Whatever combination of things it was, it brought to Swift's poetry
the same qualities that discerning writers have admired and
imitated in the prose of *A Modest Proposal* and *Gulliver's
Travels*. If, as some critics say, there are icy stretches in
the prose works of this greatest wit of his age, such as the
want of pathos, propriety, and refined "sensibilities," these
icy stretches in the poetry have troubled and discouraged
timid readers for whom it is not "poetry" at all.

By readers of all periods and persuasions, as widely di-
verse as Voltaire, Fielding, Cowper, Hazlitt, W.S. Maugham,

and Walter de la Mare, Swift's prose is described as admirable. It is prose distinguished by a concentrated, forceful clarity that springs from language tense and close-meshed. It has, indeed, the aesthetic effect of severe poetry: Professor Cleanth Brooks believes that there is more intensity in Swift's prose than in the poetry of all his contemporaries. Brooks finds greater passion in *A Modest Proposal* than in the poetry of its day. This is surely an extreme view; but if there are the same admirable qualities in both Swift's poetry and prose, it is clear that the poems have been shrugged off not because they displease, but because their ability to please comes largely from qualities associated by prejudice with prose.

Swift's limitations as a poet, then, lie in his particular virtues themselves. His remarkable intensity and conciseness, for example, may account for the lack of variety which withholds from his verse a place in the great tradition where the work of Milton and Shakespeare unquestionably stands. Recognizing his own special abilities, and feeling a predilection for parody, Swift wrote verse in his own way, just as— in his own way too—he wrote extraordinary prose.

Because it has generally been found satisfactory and easy to designate Swift as a writer of "verse," there has been for him no long-labored critical conundrum like that of "Was Pope a Poet?" Instead, the question for two centuries seems to have been whether the imprint of the devil's foot does not make Swift's poetry unfit for readers who insist upon sublimity as their sole criterion for excellence. That question, with which this book has been concerned, was long ago answered in a line by Byron: "Peace to Swift's faults! his wit hath made them pass..."

APPENDIX

ELIOT, HARDY, JOYCE, YEATS,
AND THE GHOST OF SWIFT

T.S. Eliot's *Prufrock*, 1917, and *Poems*, 1920, established
a fashion of wit and satire in modern verse; and his *Homage
to John Dryden*, 1924, invited modern readers to reconsider
the connotations of "wit" and "satire" as prejudices of
Victorian taste. His "Morning at the Window," with its dreary
basement kitchens, curbs, and gates, is somewhat reminiscent
of Swift's gray-faced parody called "A Description of the
Morning." In his "Lines for an Old Man" Eliot makes a truly
Swiftian statement of hissing wit, tiger-like irritability, and
hate for dullards. An intentional echoing of Swift may be
found in Eliot's *Four Quartets*, in the second part of "Little
Gidding," praised by W.H. Auden as the best imitation of
Dante in English. It describes the meeting, before daybreak,
with a half-familiar ghost that speaks bitterly and ironically
of "gifts" old age will bring. This ghost, says B. Rajan in
a study of the *Quartets*, may be Dante, Mallarmé, and Arnaut
Daniel compounded and "will provide the backbone for one
hundred American theses..." But the American theses, when
they are written, will have to identify the ghost with Jonathan Swift. It is in Swift's own poetry that we have first encountered Eliot's indignant phrases describing the hopeless-
ness of rage at follies that are human, the laceration of empty

laughter, and the sting of approval that comes from fools.

In acknowledging this reference to Swift in "Little Gidding" as a conscious one, Mr. Eliot adds that it is a reference which associates Swift with W.B. Yeats.* Rather harshly, Yeats himself once directed at Eliot the precise criticism so often applied to Swift. Eliot, he said, produces his effects by rejection of rhythms and metaphors familiar in romantic verse. To Yeats as a critic, what passed for novelty in Eliot's poetry was really only an unimaginative absence of the conventional; and he fell back into Victorian distinctions by calling Eliot a satirist, not a poet. Yet these very limitations, which are also those of Swift's poetry, account for much of the enthusiastic critical acceptance Eliot has met elsewhere. Among younger poets, especially, satire like Eliot's is considered a proper vehicle for serious poetic communication. W.H. Auden was recently commended by Stephen Spender (according to the New York *Times*) as the most intellectual poet of importance since Pope. Most Georgian or Victorian poets would have been distressed by such a comparison.

Among recent writers whose reputations are already great, Hardy, Joyce, and Yeats himself sometimes showed a predilection for a style that seems Swiftian. Thomas Hardy's deliberately unadorned, disillusioned poetry often unconsciously resembles Swift's. The two poets shared a dry, satiric sense of humor, they both liked homely subjects, and they wrote some of their most characteristic verses in the form of monologue and dialogue. In "A Necessitarian's Epitaph" Hardy characteristically sets down a complaint against a stupid world in what seems the bare language of speech, with an un-"poetic," Swiftian simile that likens the meaningless dance of life to the painful jig of a cat that has stepped on hot bricks. And both poets used contrast and sudden juxtapositions of the formal and colloquial or the permanent and fleeting.

Similarities might be expected in the poetry of Jonathan Swift and James Joyce, both Dublin men. Joyce's *Chamber Music* and *Pomes Penyeach*, however, are composed of liquid, mellifluous imagist verses; and it is only in his longer poems,

*In a letter to the present writer, dated June 27, 1947.

"The Holy Office," 1904, and "Gas from a Burner," 1912, privately printed in broadsides like eighteenth-century lampoons, that his lines are truly Swiftian.* Written in octosyllabic couplets, satiric and allusive, these two poems seem intentionally Swiftian with their rhymes of "give"/"Purgative," "arses"/"Katharsis," and "thumb"/"bum." They allude to Dublin drabs and giddy dames unchanged since they showed their faces in "The Journal of a Modern Lady" and "The Progress of Beauty." Using excretory imagery like Swift's, Joyce has the reverend speaker in "The Holy Office" refer to himself as a "sewer" carrying the "filthy streams" of confessions. And the conclusion of "Gas from a Burner," by substitution of a single word, "bum," turns Catholic ritual into bawdy parody, just as Swift made the conventional become surprising by an unexpected word in his parodies. It was of course not in his poetry but in his remarkable *Finnegans Wake* that Joyce made most use of Swift, punning in a hundred ways on his name and on names connected with his.

More specifically than in the poetry of Hardy and Joyce, Swift's influence can be pointed out in the work of W.B. Yeats, who once said that Swift seemed always nearby, haunting him. It is generally agreed that Yeats's best poetry is the bony, strong, almost bawdy work of his last years, when he unquestionably wrote with Swift in mind. In his "Blood and the Moon" and "The Seven Sages" he identified Swift, Burke, Goldsmith, and Berkeley with the great days of Ireland, the days he wished, through poetry at least, to recall. These glorious Irishmen, he said, were enemies of Whiggery and stood as symbols of patriotism: they still haunt the "half-dead" tower that stands for modern Ireland. Wishing especially to identify himself with Swift, he worked the phrase "saeva indignatio" into the pattern of his "Blood and the Moon," wrote a new version of Swift's epitaph from which that Latin phrase is taken, and turned from a style reminiscent of Shelley to one anti-heroic, cynical, and savage.

*The origin of the title Chamber Music was certainly Swiftian in nature, however. See Herbert Gorman, James Joyce.

Before Yeats's time there had been curious observations
on that epitaph which begins:

HIC DEPOSITUM EST CORPUS
JONATHAN SWIFT, S.T.D.
HUIUS ECCLESIAE CATHEDRALIS
DECANI,
UBI SAEVA INDIGNATIO
ULTERIUS COR LACERARE NEQUIT.

Thackeray said he had no love for a man who "chisels his
indignation on his tomb-stone, as if to perpetuate his protest
against being born of our race..." And Leslie Stephen saw
in Swift's epitaph "the last of those terrible phrases which
cling to our memory whenever his name is mentioned." Yeats
was attracted to these terrible phrases, and he made three
renderings of them in English. On January 28, 1930, Lady
Gregory wrote in her journal that she had that day copied two
versions of Yeats's translation to send to G.B. Shaw, who had
spoken of the project as a fine idea.   The first rendering,
which Lady Gregory preferred, speaks of the savage indignation which can no longer lacerate Swift's "soul." The
second rendering, and the one Lady Gregory says Yeats liked
better, substitutes "heart" for "soul." But in still another
version, published in 1931 and used in the *Collected Poems*
of Yeats, there are further variations; and here it is Swift's
"breast" that cannot be lacerated.

This final version appeared in the Introduction to *The
Words Upon the Window-Pane,* a one-act play first performed
in 1930. It is a play about a meeting of the "Dublin Spirit-
ualists' Association," who have gathered in a house that two
hundred years before had belonged to friends of Stella: a
house that has lines from a poem cut upon a window-pane.
John Corbet, described as a Cambridge undergraduate, acts
as Yeats's spokesman in the play, and it is he who recog-
nizes the words on the window as those from a poem Stella
is supposed to have written for Swift's fifty-fourth birthday:

You taught how I might youth prolong
By knowing what is right and wrong,

How from my heart to bring supplies
Of lustre to my fading eyes.

Swift, who may himself have written those lines, dominates
the play: throughout the séance that is the occasion for the
meeting, with businesslike Mrs. Henderson as the medium and
a dead child named Lulu as control, throughout the necessary
hymn-singing, and throughout Mrs. Mallet's attempts to con-
verse with her drowned husband, there is the disconcerting
voice of Jonathan Swift. He appears to Mrs. Henderson as a
horrible, dirty old ghost wearing spectacles; and his interference, violent and disturbing, brings the séance to an end.
And when the play itself is ended, one is left with the impression that the interference of Yeats's own voice through
John Corbet, like Swift's through Mrs. Henderson, is dis-
quieting. For John Corbet, the Cambridge undergraduate, is
made to inquire whether Swift did not foresee Democracy and
the enslaving of arrogant intellects, whether he did not dread
such a future, and whether it was not for this reason he refused to beget children. Though Yeats is here adapting to his
own purposes, his wish to assume the role of Swift was
genuine.

In the Introduction to *The Words Upon the Window-Pane*
he wrote that it was now his habit to read Swift's works for
months at a time, seeking to recreate the mind of a vanished
century and use it to awaken twentieth-century Ireland. During his last decade, until his death in 1939, Yeats accomplished great poetry reminiscent of Jonathan Swift, whose
own poetry has almost never been called great. In Yeats's
"Crazy Jane" poems, for example, there are the mockeries,
rages, zest, simplicity, indignation, wit, and willingness to
be ridiculous that bear the name of "Swiftian." In "Crazy
Jane and the Bishop" there is a bitter caricature of a churchman: Yeats's description of the bishop, wrinkled like the
skin of a goose's foot and hunched like a heron, has the
sound of Swift's unsparing lampoons on churchmen like Dean
Smedley.

Of all his poems, however, "Under Ben Bulben" seems
most clearly to derive from Swift. Dated September 4, 1938,

it is Yeats's counterpart to "Verses on the Death of Dr. Swift," with an admonition to surviving poets, and concluding with the three lines now inscribed on his tomb. "Horseman, pass by," Yeats's epitaph commands, in conscious imitation of Swift's own *"Abi, viator,"* "Go traveler," carved in the black stone in St. Patrick's Cathedral.

CHRONOLOGY

(Titles of Swift's chief prose works are printed in italics; titles of his chief poems appear within quotation marks.)

1667 (Nov. 30)	Jonathan Swift born in Dublin
1674-82	At Kilkenny Grammar School
1682-86	At Trinity College, Dublin
1689-99	Intermittent residence with Sir William Temple at Moor Park, Surrey
1692	M.A., Hart Hall, Oxford; "Ode to the Athenian Society"
1695	Ordained Anglican priest in Ireland
1696-98	*A Tale of a Tub* and *The Battle of the Books* written at Moor Park (published 1704)
1699	Chaplain to Lord Berkeley in Ireland
1700	Prebend of St. Patrick's Cathedral, Dublin; *Letters of Sir William Temple,* I and II (ed. Swift; third vol. in 1703)
1701	D.D. of Dublin; "Mrs. Harris's Petition" (published 1709)
1701-14	Intermittent residence in England
1709	"Baucis and Philemon"; "A Description of the Morning"
1710	Writes for the Tory *Examiner;* "A Description of a City Shower"
1710-13	Writes *Journal to Stella*

1711	*Miscellanies in Prose and Verse; The Conduct of the Allies*
1713	Membership in Scriblerus Club; installed as Dean of St. Patrick's Cathedral; "Cadenus and Vanessa" (published 1726)
1714	"The Author upon Himself" (published 1735)
1719	"On Stella's Birth-Day" (published 1727)
1720	*Proposal for the Universal Use of Irish Manufactures;* "To Stella, Who Collected and Transcribed His Poems" (published 1727); "To Stella, Visiting Me in My Sickness" (published 1727)
1721	*Letter to a Young Gentleman, Lately Enter'd into Holy Orders;* "Stella's Birth-Day" (published 1727)
1722	"A Satirical Elegy" (published 1764); "The Progress of Marriage" (published 1765); "To Stella on Her Birth-Day" (published 1766)
1723	Death of Vanessa; "Stella's Birth-Day" (published 1727); "Stella at Wood-Park" (published 1735)
1724	*The Drapier's Letters;* "To Stella" (published 1765)
1725	"Stella's Birth-Day" (published 1727); "A Receipt to Restore Stella's Youth" (published 1735)
1726	Visits Pope at Twickenham; *Gulliver's Travels*
1727	*Miscellanies,* I and II (ed. Pope); "Stella's Birth-Day"; "Holyhead Journal" (published 1882)
1728-30	Three visits to Sir Arthur and Lady Acheson at Market Hill, Ireland

1728   Death of Stella; "Last" vol. of *Miscel-
                lanies* (ed. Pope); *A Short View of the
                State of Ireland;* "My Lady's Lamenta-
                tion" (published 1765)

1729   *A Modest Proposal;* "The Journal of a
                Modern Lady"; "The Grand Question
                Debated" (published 1732)

1730   "The Lady's Dressing-Room" (published
                1732); "Death and Daphne" (published
                1735)

1731   "The Place of the Damn'd"; "A Beauti-
                ful Young Nymph Going to Bed" (pub-
                lished 1734); "Strephon and Chloe" (pub-
                lished 1734); "Verses on the Death of
                Dr. Swift" (published 1739); "The Day
                of Judgement" (exact date of composi-
                tion unknown, published 1774)

1732   "Third" vol. of *Miscellanies* (ed. Pope);
                *An Examination of Certain Abuses, Cor-
                ruptions, and Enormities in the City of
                Dublin;* "The Beasts Confession" (pub-
                lished 1738)

1733   "On Poetry: A Rapsody"; "An Epistle
                to a Lady"; *A Serious and Useful Scheme,
                to Make an Hospital for Incurables*

1735   *Works of J.S.D.D.D.S.P.D.,* four vols.
                (Dublin, published Faulkner; later ex-
                tended to twenty vols.; poetry chiefly in
                Vol. II); "Fifth" vol. of *Miscellanies*
                (ed. Pope)

1736   "The Legion Club"

1738   *Polite Conversation*

1742   Guardians appointed for Swift

1744   Death of Pope

1745 (Oct. 19) Death of Swift in Dublin

1746   "A Cantata" published

1754-55   *Works of Jonathan Swift, D.D.,* six vols.
                (London, ed. Hawkesworth; later extended,
                by Deane Swift and Nichols, to twenty-
                seven vols.); includes poems

1814   *Works of Jonathan Swift, D.D.,* nineteen
                vols. (Edinburgh, ed. Sir Walter Scott;
                second edition, corrected, in 1824); in-
                cludes poems

1833-34   *Poetical Works of Jonathan Swift,* three
                vols. (London, Aldine Edition, based on
                Scott, 1824, with "Life of Swift" by Mit-
                ford)

1910   *Poems of Jonathan Swift, D.D.,* two vols.
                (London, ed. W.E. Browning, based on
                Scott, 1824)

1937   *Poems of Jonathan Swift,* three vols.
                (Oxford, ed. Williams; text printed "from
                manuscript, from a first edition, or from
                an authoritative early text")

INDEX

141